The Best Of The Mailbox®

Learning Centers

Primary

Editor In Chief:
Marge Michel

Editors:
Diane Badden
Cynthia Holcomb
Laurel Robinson
Kathy Wolf

Artists:
Jennifer T. Bennett
Pam Crane
Sheila Krill
Rob Mayworth
Barry Slate

Cover Design:
Jim Counts

www.themailbox.com

About This Book

The Best Of The Mailbox® *Learning Centers Primary* is a collection of the best learning centers published in the Primary editions of *The Mailbox*® from 1988 to 1994. It is designed to provide an extensive collection of skill-specific, teacher-created, easy-to-make learning centers for today's busy teacher. The learning centers include illustrations, complete instructions, and corresponding reproducible patterns.

©1996 by THE EDUCATION CENTER, INC.
All rights reserved.

ISBN# 1-56234-150-2

Manufactured in the United States

10 9 8 7 6 5

Table Of Contents

Fold-A-Flash-Cards

These rhyme-reinforcing flash cards are easy to make and fun for students to use. To construct each card, cut a triangle and fold as shown. Glue pictures on each corner, programming one of the pictures on the bottom corner to rhyme with the picture on the top. The student looks at the picture on top, selects the matching rhyme, and then unfolds the corner to check. If he is correct, the student will find a smiley face inside the flap.

Margaret Maxwell
Oregon City, OR

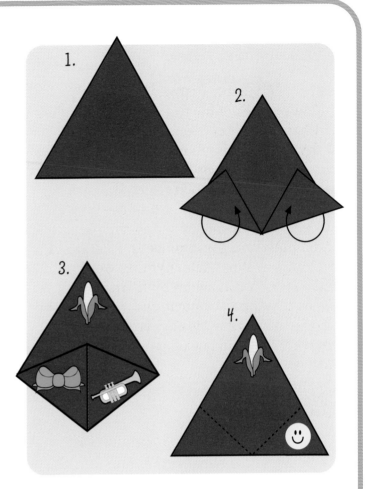

The Radish Patch

Take your students to the radish patch for practice with rhyming words. To construct a file-folder vegetable patch, decorate the front of a manila folder to resemble a garden. On the inside, draw a vegetable plot, then use an X-acto® knife to create several small slits in each row as shown. Insert a paper clip into each slit. Next, program radish-shaped cards with words that can be sorted into rhyming pairs, and code for self-checking. Place the folder in a center. A student finds each pair of rhyming words, and clips them to the vegetable plot. Watch the garden grow with rows of rhyming radishes!

Debbie Smith
Port Jervis, NY

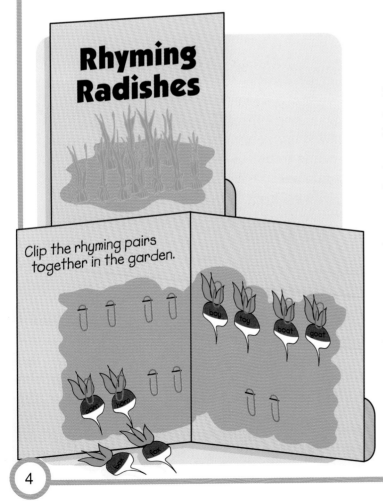

Rhyme-Time Puzzles

This puzzle center for beginning readers will help students piece together a review of rhyming words. To create a puzzle, use a small paper plate or Styrofoam® tray and cut into two puzzle-piece sections. Write a rhyming word on each half of the puzzle. Store pieces for five or six puzzles in a zippered plastic bag and place in a center. A student matches each rhyming word pair, and checks his answers by fitting the pieces together. For variation, program the puzzles with pictures of rhyming words or program for a review of synonyms or antonyms.

Fran Petersen
North Tonawanda, NY

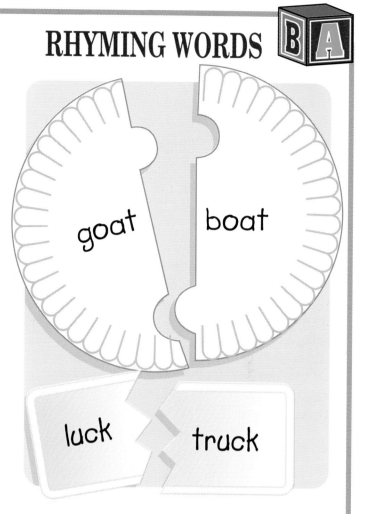

Doughnut Delight

Tempt your students to practice rhyming-word skills with this mouth-watering center! To make the center, program doughnut-shaped cutouts with words to be sorted into rhyming pairs, and code the back of each cutout for self-checking. Fill an empty doughnut box with the cutouts and place in a center. A student sorts the doughnuts into rhyming pairs, then turns over the cutouts to check his work. What a tasty way to reinforce rhymes!

Diane Vogel
Chamblee, GA

BA SIGHT WORDS

Sight-Word Partner Puzzle

Fill a center with sight-word puzzles and watch student partners make the pieces fall into place! To make a puzzle, cut apart a seasonal or thematic shape into the desired number of pieces. Program each piece with a sight word and place the assembled puzzle in a center. Each student takes a turn reading a word from a puzzle piece, and may remove the piece if his partner confirms that he read the word correctly. After all the pieces have been removed from the puzzle, the partners work together to reconstruct the puzzle, reading the word on each piece as it is put into place.

Ann Price
Ridgeway, VA

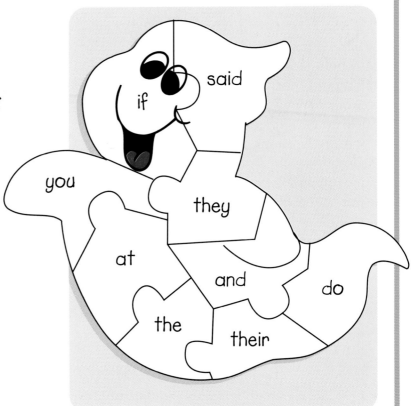

Gone Fishin'

The catch of the day is a sight-word review that will hook student interest! Set up a center with a fishbowl, construction-paper fish cutouts programmed with sight words, and a small fishing pole. Attach a paper clip to the mouth of each fish cutout before placing into the fishbowl, and fasten a magnet to the end of the fishing pole's string. Students work in pairs as they take turns dropping the line into the bowl to "reel in" a fish. The student reads the word programmed on his catch, and may keep it if he is correct. The student who collects the most fish is declared "First-Rate Fisherman."

Rachel Carter

The ABCs Of Me!

1. Aa	14. Nn
2. Bb	15. Oo
3. Cc	16. Pp
4. Dd	17. Qq
5. Ee	18. Rr
6. Ff	19. Ss
7. Gg	20. Tt
8. Hh	21. Uu
9. Ii	22. Vv
10. Jj	23. Ww
11. Kk	24. Xx
12. Ll	25. Yy
13. Mm	26. Zz

1. Write the letters of the alphabet on a sheet of paper.

2. After each letter write something that you like that begins with that letter.

The ABCs Of Me

Here's a great back-to-school center that promotes self-esteem and confidence. Label the inside of a file folder with the letters of the alphabet, and laminate. Using a wipe-off marker, the student writes things he likes which begin with each alphabet letter. An alternative to laminating would be to ask students to write the letters on a separate sheet of paper. Provide time for students to share their favorites with their teacher or class.

Carolyn Barwick
Madison Heights, MI

Alphabet Pop-up Book

This class-created alphabet booklet will stand out above the rest. After reading aloud the story *The Z Was Zapped* by Chris Van Allsburg, place a set of small, tagboard, alphabet letters for tracing in a container at a center. Have each student draw a letter from the container, trace and cut out the letter from construction paper, then place his tagboard tracer in a second container. (This will guarantee that each student uses a different alphabet letter.) Next have each student write an action sentence describing his letter on a piece of scrap paper.

To make a booklet page, a student folds in half an 8 1/2" x 11" sheet of paper and cuts two slits near the center of the fold as shown. (Give assistance as needed.) He then opens the folded paper and glues his letter cutout to the protruding portion. Next he copies his action sentence onto the page, then decorates the page to show the action being described. Compile the pages in alphabetical order and bind into a class booklet for all to enjoy.

Chris Crane
Olney Elementary School
Northwood, OH

NO!

A

The A answered angrily.

Instructions: 2" 1 1/2" 8 1/2"

Hands-On Alphabetizing

Students stock up on alphabetizing skills at this high-interest center! In a large cardboard box, place a number of classroom items for alphabetizing (such as a book, a crayon, a dictionary, a pencil, a ruler, and an eraser). Create an answer key, enclose it in an envelope, and place it in the box. A student removes the items, arranges them in ABC order on a table, and uses the answer key to check his work. (Be sure to discuss the possibility of alternative orders due to the different names items can be called, such as *binder* and *notebook*.)

If desired, place an empty box in the classroom and invite students to bring clean, discarded items from home for use in the center. Then, periodically, empty your center box and restock it with several of these items and a corresponding answer key.

LaDawn Rhodes
Shelton Park Elementary
Virginia Beach, VA

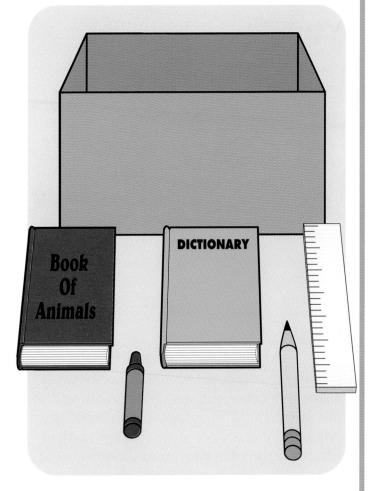

The Magic Picture Show

A little bit of magic goes a long way toward improving alphabetizing skills! Cut a colorful, 8" x 10" picture from a magazine; then glue it to an 8" x 10" piece of poster board. Cut the picture into 10 to 12 horizontal strips. As you cut, print a word on the back of each strip, making sure the words are in alphabetical order from the top strip to the bottom strip (see illustration). Store the strips in an empty box. A child removes the strips and places the words in alphabetical order in the box. To check his work, he turns over the strips one at a time. If the strips are in correct order, a picture will "magically" appear. For younger students, label the strips with letters to sequence.

Cookie-Sheet Sequencing

Make sequencing practice a manipulative treat! Label a set of cookie-shaped cutouts with words to alphabetize. On the back of each cutout, place a piece of magnetic tape. Store the cutouts with an answer key in a Ziploc® bag. The student removes the cutouts from the bag and places them in alphabetical order on a cookie sheet. If desired, store several sets of color-coded cutouts and answer keys in the same bag. Students sort the cutouts by color, then alphabetize them.

Vickie Simpson—Gr. 1
Eastwood Elementary School
Big Rapids, MI

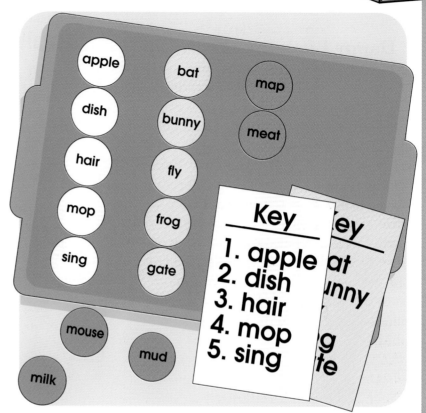

The Stockings Were Hung

Give sequencing practice a seasonal flair at this manipulative center. Mount the fireplace (pattern on page 65) on the inside of a file folder; then program with directions. Decorate the front of the folder as desired. Cut seven stocking shapes from the pattern on page 66. Program the shapes with words to alphabetize. Or write a sentence or phrase on each from "The Night Before Christmas" by Clement Moore. (Display a copy of the poem for reference.) Laminate all pieces for durability. Store the cutouts in a Press-On Pocket attached to the back of the folder. A student removes the cutouts and places them in sequential order on the fireplace mantel. Happy Christmas!

Tonya Byrd—Gr. 2
F.J. Delaine Elementary
Wedgefield, SC

Happy Birthday, Mr. Braille

Create this hands-on activity in celebration of Louis Braille's birthday (January 4). At a center place a copy of the braille alphabet (page 67), a large container of dried peas, 3" x 12" strips of construction paper, and glue. Using the displayed alphabet as a reference, have each youngster create a word by gluing peas onto a strip of personalized construction paper. When all projects are completely dried, display them at the center. Challenge students to decode the words by gently touching the peas and looking only at the posted alphabet.

Chris Christensen
Las Vegas, NV

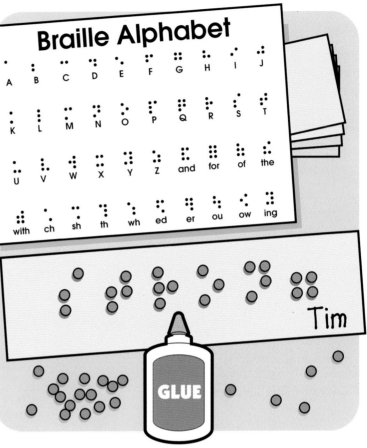

It's As Simple As A, B, C

If you're looking for a center that reinforces a variety of skills and is easy to make, then look no farther! Cut 13 index cards in half. Label each card with a letter of the alphabet; then place the cards in a Press-On Pocket attached to the inside of a laminated file folder. Use a wipe-off marker to program the file folder with directions such as:

— Arrange letter cards in alphabetical order. Write the letters on a piece of paper. Or have someone check your work.
— Make as many words as you can using the letter cards. Each letter card may be used only once. Write your words on a piece of paper.
— Take five cards from the pocket. Write the letters on a piece of paper. Now write the letters that come before and after each letter.

Wipe the folder clean and reprogram the directions as desired.

Marilyn Borden—Gr. 3
Castleton Elementary School
Bomoseen, VT

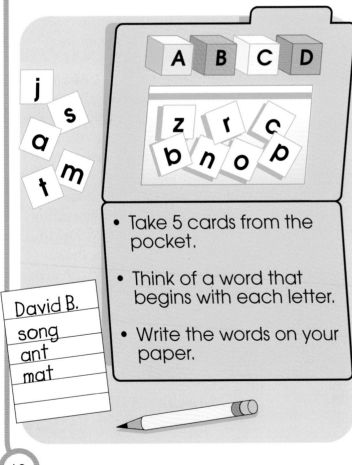

Tracking Down Blends

Your students will delight in tracking down blends at this center. Use colorful markers to program each of several 9" x 6" sheets of construction paper with a two- or three-letter blend. Place the programmed sheets in a decorated box at the center. Each student selects a sheet and writes one word on the card which begins with the blend shown. He then illustrates the word he has written. Next the student lists five or more words on the back of his card which begin with the programmed blend. Have students use dictionaries to verify their spellings. Tallyho! It's time to track down blends!

Basketful Of Practice

Collect a basketful of plastic eggs to hatch word attack practice. Using a permanent marker, write initial consonants or blends on the left half of the egg and a word-ending on the right half. Nestle the eggs in a grass-filled basket tied with a pretty bow.

A student selects an egg and rotates the left half to make new-words, pronouncing each newly formed word. Advanced students may use these words in compositions.

Judy Peterson
Delta, UT

CONTRACTIONS

Jack-O'-Lantern Contractions

For October contraction practice, display this working bulletin board. Make jack-o'-lantern cutouts with black noses and mouths (pattern on page 68). Using white chalk, write a contraction on each mouth and laminate. After attaching these cutouts to the board, insert a thumbtack where each eye should be. Provide laminated, black triangles labeled in chalk with words which correspond to the contractions. Attach a magnetic strip to the back of each eye and store them in a pocket on the board. Students complete the face of each jack-o'-lantern by matching the words to each contraction.

Deborah Mackie—Chapter 1 Reading
Granite Falls Elementary
Granite Falls, NC

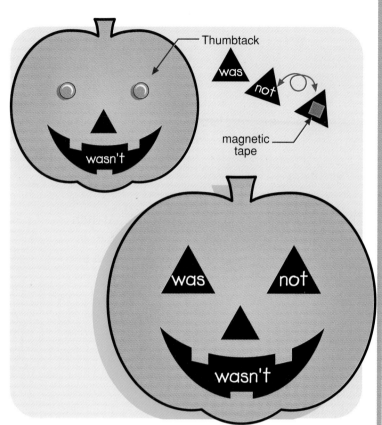

Locomotive Language Lesson

All aboard for contraction practice! Decorate the outside of a file folder with train artwork (pattern on page 69) and a title as shown. Cut out an engine and several boxcars from construction paper, and glue to the inside of the folder. Program each boxcar with a contraction. Using chalk, write the matching contraction word pairs on wheels cut from black construction paper. Laminate the folder and wheels. Store the wheels in a pocket.

To practice, a student removes the wheels from the pocket and places them below the correct boxcars.

To vary, program the center for math matching exercises.

Elizabeth Harris—ESL Teacher
Kimball Elementary School
Mesquite, TX

What's The Purpose?

Students must decide if an apostrophe is being used to separate a missing letter or letters in a contraction, or if it is being used to show possession. Label an index card *Contractions;* then write a sentence containing an underlined contraction on the card. Label another card *Possessive Nouns* and write a sentence containing an underlined possessive noun on the card. Attach each card to the front of a decorated can. On each of several craft sticks, write a sentence containing either an underlined possessive noun or an underlined contraction. Color-code the backs of the sticks for self-checking; then place the sticks and a card labeled with student directions in a resealable plastic bag at the center. A student sorts the sticks into the containers, then uses the color code on the backs of the sticks to check his work.

Punctuating With Pasta

Cook up an interest in quotation marks at this punctuation center. Place a supply of glue, markers, sentence strips, and large elbow macaroni at a center. Also display a list of sentences that have not been punctuated with the required quotation marks. A student copies each sentence onto a sentence strip, allowing room for the missing punctuation. Next he arranges macaroni pieces to represent the missing marks and glues them in place. For practice in using apostrophes and commas, use a similar technique. It's the perfect recipe for enriching your youngsters' punctuation skills!

Cheryl Sneed
Winters Elementary
Winters, TX

Brain Busters

Keep students informed about what's happening in their community and their world at this weekly current-events center. From your local newspaper, cut a variety of articles that you find appropriate for youngsters. Post the articles at the center. Make a list of the people, places, and events featured in the articles; then use the list to program a Brain Buster Task Card. (See the illustration.) Place the task card and a supply of writing paper at the center. A student uses the information in the articles to unscramble the words and/or phrases on the task card. If desired, provide an answer key for self-checking.

Jeannette Freeman—Gr. 3
Baldwin School Of Puerto Rico
Puerto Rico

Brain Buster Task Card

Have you read the latest news?
Unscramble these newsworthy people, places, and events.

1. hietW ouHse
2. dnarG yCnnao
3. tgorudh
4. lrHaily tlnnCoi
5. tatSue fO irLbyet

No Rain Expected

For A Scenic Vacation, Visit The Grand Canyon

First Lady Speaks Out

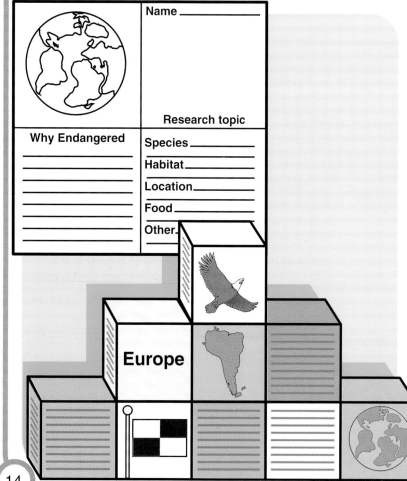

Name _____

Research topic

Why Endangered
_____
_____
_____
_____
_____

Species _____
Habitat _____
Location _____
Food _____
Other _____

Europe

Research Pyramid

Build a pyramid of research right in your classroom! After researching assigned topics, students complete duplicated research forms. Completed forms are cut apart and glued to the sides of boutique tissue boxes. Cover the tops and bottoms of the boxes with construction-paper squares. Stack the boxes in a pyramid shape at a center. Students visit the display and learn from the research their classmates have done.

Wendy Sondov—Gr. 3
St. Louis, MO

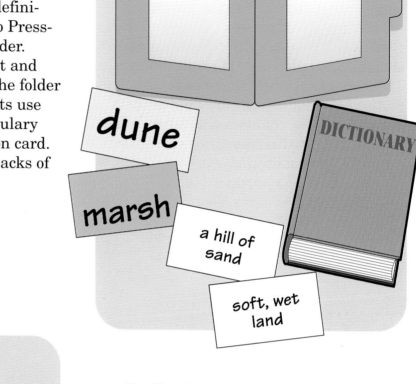

Dictionary Center

Help students get acquainted with the dictionary. Label colorful index cards with vocabulary words. Write matching definitions on white index cards. Glue two Press-On Pockets on the inside of a file folder. Store the colored cards in one pocket and the white cards in the other. Place the folder and a dictionary at a center. Students use the dictionary to look up each vocabulary word and find its matching definition card. Include an answer key or code the backs of the cards for self-checking.

Marilyn Borden—Gr. 3
Castleton Elementary School
Bomoseen, VT

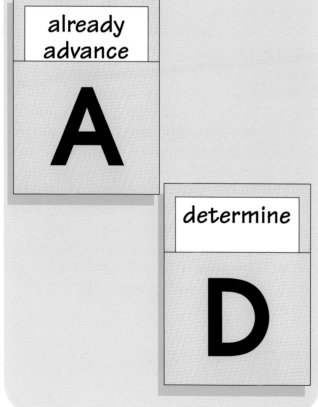

Bulletin-Board Dictionary

There are some super spellers in Augusta, Georgia, who are producing more creative stories as a result of this bulletin-board dictionary. Label a library-card pocket for each letter of the alphabet. Staple the pockets in order on a bulletin board. Cut twenty-six 3" x 8" cards, and place one in each pocket. When a student needs help spelling a word, he brings the card from the appropriate pocket to the teacher, who writes the word on the card. The student copies the word on his paper and returns the card to the pocket. Students will soon find many words they need already on the cards. This may inspire them to try a different word instead.

Tami Johnson—Gr. 3
Augusta, GA

Sizing Up Written Directions

Reinforce reading and following written directions with this hands-on activity. From several colors of 8" x 10" poster board, cut a supply of templates. (See the illustration.) On the templates, above each cut-out area, write a one-sentence direction. A student chooses a template and places it atop a 9" x 12" sheet of paper. He then reads each direction and follows it by drawing in the open area below the sentence. When he has completed both directions, he removes the template and copies the sentences above the corresponding pictures. Following written directions has never been so much fun!

Beverly Bippes—Gr. 1
Humphrey Public School
Humphrey, NE

Draw a red flag.

Draw three pink pigs.

Draw a black cow.

Draw four yellow ducks.

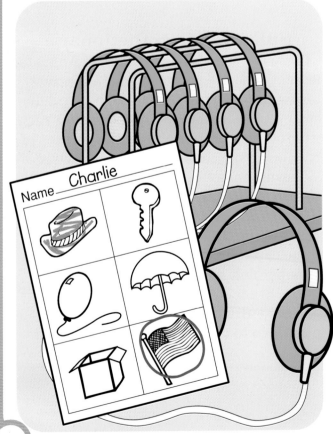

Lend An Ear

Students quickly discover that careful listening is the key to success at this following-directions center. Design an activity sheet that features several simple shapes (see illustration), then make a recording of directions that correspond to the shapes. Place the recording at a listening center along with crayons and a supply of activity sheets. A student colors the shapes by carefully following the directions provided on the recording. If desired, provide an answer key at the center so that students can check their work at the end of the recording.

Dianne Neumann—Gr. 2
Frank C. Whitely School
Hoffman Estates, IL

Hillary Hippo handed her handkerchief to Harvey.

BABY WIPES

Copy this sentence:

Hillary Hippo handed her handkerchief to Harvey.

Copy these word pairs:

clock	make	look
dock	wake	book

The Writing's On The Desk

If you have an old student desk, you've got the makings of an unusual handwriting center. Cover the desktop with lined chart paper; then place clear Con-Tact® paper over it. Label a set of colorful index cards with simple handwriting activities. Place the cards, several wipe-off markers, and a container of baby wipes inside the desk. A student comes to the desk, chooses a card, and uses one of the markers to complete the activity on the desktop. When finished, he simply wipes the desktop clean so that it's ready for the next student. The writing's on the desk—this center will be a favorite with your young writers!

Cursive Writing

Make cursive writing something special with laminated practice sheets. Write each student's name at the top of a piece of handwriting paper and laminate. Place the laminated sheets and wipe-off pens in a folder at a center. The student finds his own personalized practice sheet and uses a pen to practice writing his name. When finished, he wipes his paper clean and returns it to the folder for another day.

Jeani Z. Fullard—Gr. 2
Lealman Avenue Elementary
St. Petersburg, FL

James

James

James

BA HANDWRITING

Handwriting Across The USA

Travel across our great country with a unique handwriting center. Duplicate the reproducible containing an alphabetical list of state abbreviations (page 71.) Place the reproducible at a center with a poster showing a large, labeled United States map (page 70) and student directions. Provide an answer key and a folder for storing student work. What a great way to throw a little geography into handwriting practice!

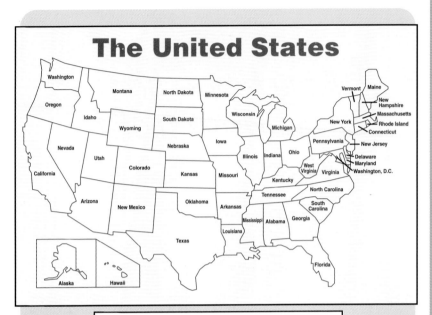

Student Directions:
1. Take a worksheet. Write your name on it.
2. Look at the map. Find the name of the state that matches the first abbreviation.
3. Write the name of the state next to its abbreviation.
4. Do this for the rest of the abbreviations.
5. When you have written all 50 states, check your list with the key, then place your paper in the folder.

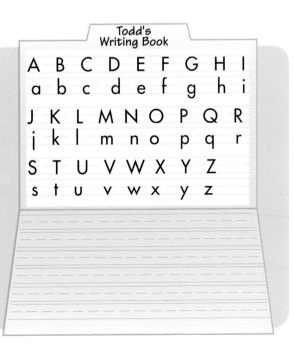

Reusable Writing Tablets

Help students improve their manuscript or cursive handwriting with reusable writing tablets. To make each tablet, write the alphabet on a piece of writing paper and glue it inside a file folder. Glue a blank piece of writing paper below the alphabet; then laminate the folder. Using a wipe-off marker, the student traces the letters shown or practices writing them on the blank sheet. Because they're laminated, the tablets can be wiped clean and used over and over again.

N. Jean Ellis—Gr. 3
Lorenzo Elementary
Lorenzo, TX

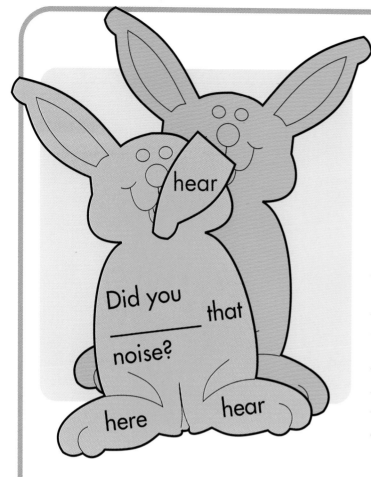

Did you _____ that noise?

hear

here   hear

WORD MEANINGS

"Hare-raising" Homophones

Get your students hopped up about homophones with these adorable bunny cutouts. Duplicate and cut out several pink, white, and tan construction-paper bunny shapes using the pattern on page 72. Program each bunny's feet with a pair of homophones; then program its body with a sentence which corresponds to one of the homophones. (Insert a blank in the sentence where the homophone should appear.) Fold down the bunny's left ear and program it with the correct answer as shown. Unfold the ears and laminate the bunny cutouts. Place the cutouts and a supply of cotton balls in a basket. A student reads the sentence on each cutout and places a cotton-ball tail near his homophone choice. He then checks his work by folding down the bunny's

Multiple Meanings

A holly-jolly time will be had at this seasonal center! Using the patterns on page 73, duplicate a supply of red berry clusters and green holly leaves. Write a word with multiple meanings on each berry cluster. Then write each meaning of the word on a separate leaf. Laminate and cut out the shapes; then use a permanent marker to program the backs of the cutouts for self-checking. Store the cutouts in a holiday basket. A student matches the holly leaves to the correct berries, then flips the cutouts to check his work. Happy holidays!

Tonya Byrd—Gr. 2
Shaw Heights Elementary
Shaw Air Force Base, SC

to bother someone

bug

an insect

to sway back and forth

a stone

rock

a type of music

BA PARTS OF SPEECH

Positively Pronouns

Here's an activity that provides noun and pronoun practice. Program the outside of a 9" x 12" string-tie envelope with a set of sentences as shown. Label a wooden craft stick with a pronoun to replace the underlined noun or nouns in each sentence. Store the labeled sticks and an answer key inside the envelope. A student completes the center by reading each sentence and placing an appropriate stick atop the underlined portion of the sentence. He then writes his sentences on a paper and checks his completed work against the answer key.

Susan L. Nixon
Avondale, AZ

Use the craft stick to change the nouns to pronouns.
1. <u>Jill</u> went to school.
2. <u>Spelling</u> is easy.
3. Give the reading book to <u>Jean and Jenny</u>.
4. <u>Bill</u> is not in school today.
5. The lost dog was <u>Jane's</u>.
6. If you find the pencil, give it to <u>Jim</u>.
7. Do not throw the ball to <u>Sally</u>.
8. <u>Mom and Dad</u> are coming home.

She

It

them.

her.

Daffy Descriptions

Tickle your youngsters' funny bones and reinforce their adjective skills with this center activity. Enlist your students' help in cutting out cartoon characters from magazines and newspapers. Place the character cutouts, a supply of 3" x 9" strips of construction paper, glue, scissors, and pencils at a center. A student glues a character cutout to the top portion of a construction-paper strip. Then below the cutout he writes a list of adjectives describing the character. Later place the completed projects at a writing center. Have each student choose a character strip, then incorporate the adjectives listed into a descriptive story.

VaReane Gray Heese—Gr. 2
Springfield Elementary
Omaha, NE

1. clever
2. hungry
3. dramatic
4. grouchy
5. funny
6. orange
7. short
8. sneaky

1. funny
2. crazy
3. zany
4. silly
5. clumsy
6. wacky
7. squawking
8. green

Noun Riddles

Reinforce noun identification through riddles! Place glue, scissors, markers, a supply of magazines, 3" x 5" cards, and standard-size envelopes at a center. A student cuts the picture of a noun from a magazine, then glues the picture onto a 3" x 5" card. Next, on the outside of an envelope, she writes a sentence that describes but does not name the noun, followed by the question "What am I?" Then she tucks her picture card inside her envelope. When each student has completed the center, punch a hole in the upper left-hand corner of each envelope; then collate the envelopes on a ring. (Laminate the envelopes and cards for durability if desired.) Return the collection of noun riddles to the center. A student reads and answers each riddle, then checks her answer by peeking at the picture card inside the envelope.

adapted from an idea by Johnna Langwell—Gr. 2
Anderson Elementary
Bronson, MI

I have bark but I can't bite.
What am I?

Common Or Proper?

Clear up questions about common and proper nouns with this bookmaking activity. Label one piece of construction paper for each alphabet letter by writing the uppercase form and the lowercase form on opposite sides. Students complete one or more pages by gluing magazine pictures or sketching drawings of common nouns on the lowercase pages and proper nouns on the uppercase pages. When all letter pages are complete, bind them together to form a class book.

Marilyn Borden—Gr. 3
Castleton Elementary School
Bomoseen, VT

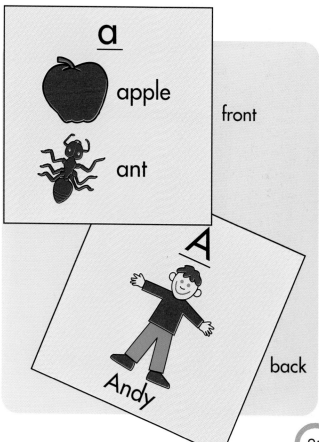

B A PARTS OF SPEECH

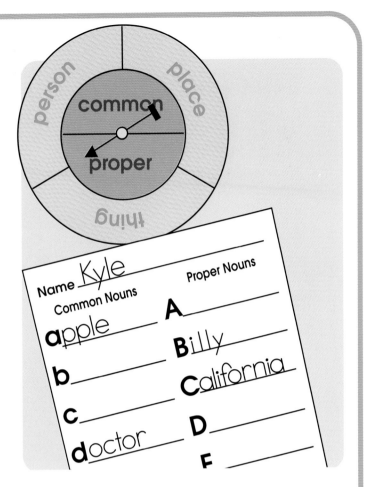

Noun Spin-off

Take a spin with common and proper nouns! To create a game wheel, visually divide an 8-inch tagboard circle into halves and a 12-inch tagboard circle into thirds. Label the smaller circle "common" and "proper." Center and glue the smaller circle atop the larger one; then label the larger circle "person," "place," and "thing." Laminate the game wheel; then attach a spinner to the center of the wheel. Place the game wheel and a supply of student activity sheets (see illustration) at a center. A student spins the spinner to determine the type of noun; then he spins again to determine a category. He then writes a corresponding noun on his activity sheet. Have students store their activity sheets in a folder at the center and complete them during several sittings, or have students complete their activity sheets with partners.

adapted from an idea by Marilyn Borden—Gr. 3
Castleton Elementary School
Bomoseen, VT

Season's Greetings

Reinforce noun and verb skills with holiday cards. Enlist the help of your youngsters in collecting an assortment of holiday cards ready for recycling. Cut away the inside of each card; then place the card fronts, a supply of 3" x 9" strips of white construction paper, and a supply of 9" x 12" sheets of colorful construction paper at a center. A student attaches the card of his choice and two paper strips to a sheet of construction paper as shown. After labeling the strips "Nouns" and "Verbs," he lists words on the strips that correspond to the card. Happy holidays!

Geraldine Caughell—Gr. 2
Landis Elementary, Logansport, IN

pre-

re-

mis-

dis-

Name _____ Pam

pre-
precut

re-
redo

mis-
mislead

dis-
disable

Prefix Practice

Students wholeheartedly pursue words containing prefixes at this center. Trace four heart shapes from page 74 onto poster board. Laminate; then use a wipe-off marker to program each heart with a prefix. Trace four heart shapes onto a master and duplicate student copies. Place the copies, the poster, and a dictionary at the center. A student labels a paper to match the poster, then lists words in each heart outline that have the appropriate prefixes. When all students have completed the center, compile their word lists, and discuss any errors. Reprogram the poster with more prefixes. Or program the poster with suffixes or vowel sounds.

Marilyn Borden—Gr. 3
Castleton Elementary School
Bomoseen, VT

Prefix Pinups

Students hang out their vocabulary skills at this center. Suspend a length of clothesline between two table or desk legs. Program each of several wooden spring-type clothespins with a vocabulary word containing a prefix. Program light-colored fabric squares with matching definitions. Store the clothespins and fabric squares in a basket. A student clips the fabric squares to the clothesline by matching the programming. To further challenge students, have them suspend the words in alphabetical order by their root words.

unhappy rebuild untied dishonest

not happy   build again   not tied   not honest

not tied

untied

CREATIVE THINKING

Red-Hot Riddles

Perfect for the valentine season, this center project encourages creative thinking. Using the patterns on page 75, make a heart template from tagboard; then duplicate student copies of the box art onto white construction paper. Place these items along with a supply of 9" x 12" red construction paper, glue, scissors, pencils, and markers or crayons at a center. Once a student has chosen a red object and brainstormed four clues about the object, he is ready to begin the activity.

To begin, a student cuts out a copy of the box art; then he illustrates and labels his red object in the center square of the cutout. Next he folds one flap over his illustration. On the back of this flap, he writes a one-sentence clue about his illustration. He continues in this manner until each flap has been folded and labeled. Next the student folds a sheet of red construction paper in half and then in half again. He places the template atop the folded paper as directed on the pattern, traces the template, and cuts on the outlines. After unfolding and opening the resulting heart cutout, the student attaches his riddle project to the center of the heart as shown. For a red-hot display, mount the completed projects on a bulletin board for all to enjoy.

Darlene LaFrance, G.S. Paine School, Brockton, MA

an apple

It grows on trees.

Place on fold

Place on fold

Fairy Tale Puzzle

Whisk your students off to the land of fairy tales with this matching activity. Label the top halves of large cards with fairy tale titles. Write sentences describing events from the fairy tales on the card bottoms. Cut apart tops and bottoms of the cards and store in an envelope. Students read the cards and make fairy tale matches.

Rhonda Thurman-Rice, Catoosa, OK

Cinderella

A fairy godmother helps a poor girl go to the ball.

Sentence Shenanigans

Reviewing subjects and predicates can lead to some pretty silly sentence shenanigans. Working from a list of descriptive sentences, program one set of sentence strips with the sentence subjects and a second set with the sentence predicates. (Use one color of sentence strips for subjects and another for predicates so that the strips are easily identifiable.) Tuck the strips in a Ziploc® bag; then place the bag and a supply of paper, pencils, and crayons at a center. A student removes the strips from the bag and randomly pairs each subject strip with a predicate strip. After reading each of the sentences he has created, the student chooses the sentence he thinks is the silliest. He then copies and illustrates that sentence on a sheet of paper.

Marilyn Borden—Gr. 3
Castleton Elementary School, Bomoseen, VT

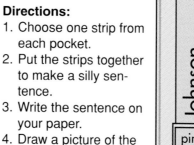

The tall, strong farmer takes ballet lessons.

Silly Sentences

Giggles, chuckles, and sentence structure practice all take place at this center! Cut each of three differently colored sheets of 9" x 12" construction paper into eight strips (each strip measures 1 1/2" x 9"). Program one set of colored strips with a variety of subjects, another set with a variety of predicates, and the final set with a variety of prepositional phrases. Store each set of colored strips in a pocket attached to the inside of a file folder. The student chooses one strip from each pocket and creates a silly sentence to copy and illustrate. For an added delight, include the names of teachers, the principal, or other school staff on the subject cards!

Shelly Johnson—Gr. 3, Choteau, MT

Directions:
1. Choose one strip from each pocket.
2. Put the strips together to make a silly sentence.
3. Write the sentence on your paper.
4. Draw a picture of the sentence.

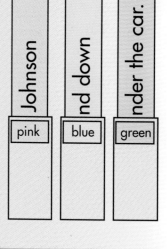

Johnson — pink
nd down — blue
nder the car. — green

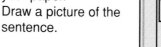

Mr. Shopbell | ate a banana | in the middle of the night.

SPELLING

Say, Spell, And Peek

Help students recognize and spell CVC words with this set of movable cards. Cut ten 2" x 8" tagboard strips and ten 2" x 4" tagboard strips. Draw a CVC word picture on half of each large card; then write the CVC word on the remaining half. Place smaller cards over the written CVC words and attach with brad fasteners. Students name the pictures, spell the words, and check their answers by "peeking" under the smaller cards. Or laminate the cards and have students write their answers on the blank cards with wipe-off markers before checking.

Dianne Knight
Stratton Elementary School
Madison, TN

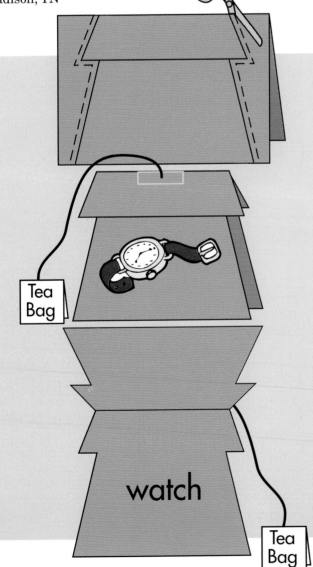

Spelling Is My Cup Of Tea

To brew up lots of spelling practice, cut out several tea bag shapes from folded tagboard as shown. Glue a picture on the outside of each tea bag. On the inside, write the picture's name. Tape a piece of string to each tea bag. Place several tea bags and instructions in a Ziploc® bag. Store all the Ziploc® bags in a folder labeled "Spelling Is My Cup Of Tea." The student takes a bag from the folder, looks at the picture on each tea bag, and writes the word on his paper. To check, the student opens the tea bag to reveal the spelling.

Viola Gardner, Bertrand, NE

Magnetic Spelling

Magnetic manipulatives attract student pairs to this spelling-reinforcement center. Using two differently colored markers (one for vowel letters and another for consonant letters), write the spelling words for the week on word cards. Cut the cards apart, separating the letters in each word; then attach magnetic tape to the back of each letter. Group the consonant and vowel letters; then place each group of letters in an appropriately labeled container. Cover the back portions of two metal kitchen pads with decorative Con-tact® paper. Place the pads, the containers, and a spelling list at a center. Each student takes a metal pad; then, taking turns, the students use the letters to spell the words their partners call out.

Peggy Plemmons—Varying Exceptionalities
Normandy Village Elementary School #221
Jacksonville, FL

Scrambled Egg Spelling

Give spelling practice a new look at this seasonal center. Number and write weekly spelling words on individual slips of paper, scrambling the letters of each word. Place each strip inside a plastic egg; then place the eggs in an Easter basket. Students open the eggs, then unscramble the letters to correctly spell the words on their papers. Duplicate a numbered answer sheet similar to the one shown and provide an answer key for self-checking if desired.

Carol Gravelle
Warsaw Central School, Warsaw, NY

Shamrock Synonyms

It's no blarney! A treasure of synonyms awaits your students. Challenge students to list synonym pairs on a large sheet of paper displayed at a center. Have students check the list for duplications before adding their contributions. After a week or two, place a shamrock tracer (pattern on page 76) and green construction paper at the center. Proof the list for spelling errors; then instruct students to transfer a predetermined number of synonym pairs (divide the pairs equally among students) onto shamrock cutouts. When all pairs are listed, arrange the shamrock cutouts into one large shamrock! 'Tis a sight to behold!

Rosemary Kavner—Gr. 2
Elizabeth Lenz, Reno, NV

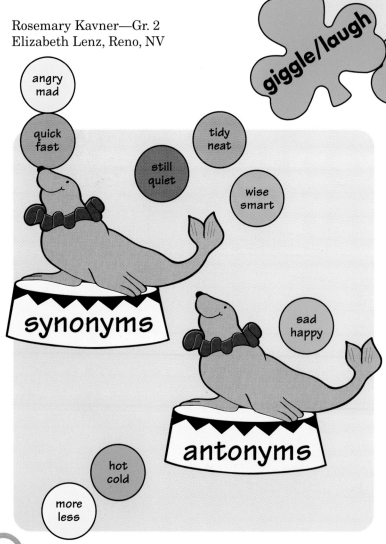

Shamrock Synonyms

Mrs. Smith

2nd Grade

giggle/laugh   run/jog   home/house

angry mad

quick fast

still quiet

tidy neat

wise smart

synonyms

sad happy

antonyms

hot cold

more less

Having A Ball

This show must go on! Use this versatile center to reinforce a variety of skills. Create two seal cutouts using the pattern on page 77. Also cut a supply of colorful circles from construction paper. Program the cutouts for a sorting activity such as antonyms and synonyms, questions and statements, or true and false facts. If desired, program the backs of the cutouts for self-checking before laminating them for durability. Place the cutouts at a center. A student sorts each circle cutout to the appropriate seal as shown. Now that's a class act!

m br
f at
p r c b

b t l f sh st
m ake

Words-Go-Round

These carousel horse tachisto-scopes make word-family practice a merry experience. Duplicate the horse pattern (page 78) on tagboard. Color each pattern; then program each saddle with a common word ending such as -ack, -at, or -ate. For each horse, program a 1" x 18" tagboard "pole" with corresponding initial consonants, blends, or di-graphs. Laminate all pieces for durability; then cut them out. Slit each saddle along the dotted lines and insert the corresponding "pole." For a carousel display, staple the ends of each pole to a bulletin board. A student slides each horse up and down its pole as he reads each word shown. Whee!

Tina Genay, Great Bend, PA

What's My Sound?

This center takes only a minute to make, and it's great vowel practice for individuals or small groups! Label three plastic cups with the different sounds of *ea*. Place the cups and a pre-pared set of *ea* word cards in the center. Children sound out the word cards and sort them into the correct cups. Code the cards for self-checking. This activity can be adapted for other vowel practice and a variety of read-ing and math skills.

Cindy Ward
Yellow Branch School
Rustburg, VA

bread ĕ

team ē

great ā

steak

thread

each

VOWEL SOUNDS

Colorful Gobblers

Featherless fowl become colorful gobblers at this vowel center! Gather an assortment of plastic clothespins in five different colors; then create a color code like the one shown to correspond to your clothespin collection. Mount the turkey head pattern from page 79 near the center of a nine-inch poster-board circle. Program the perimeter of the circle with desired words and color-code the back of the cutout for self-checking. Create a desired number of featherless fowl; then laminate the cutouts for durability. Place the clothespins (in a resealable plastic bag), the color code, and the circles at a center. Using the color code as his guide, a student attaches clothespins (feathers) to a cutout to indicate the appropriate vowel sounds of the words shown. Then he flips the cutout to check his work. When the entire flock has feathers, his job is done!

Color Code
red=ĕ   orange=ŏ
blue=ē   green=ō
yellow=ī

Pocketing Vowel Sounds

Reinforce short- and long-vowel sounds with this hands-on activity. You will need a pocket poster for each vowel. To make a poster, attach an equal number of library-card pockets to each side of a piece of colorful poster board. Label one side of the poster for the short sound and the opposite side for the long sound. Next make a set of corresponding cards for each poster. To do this, mount pictures cut from discarded student workbooks onto small index cards (one card per pocket). If desired, code the backs of the cards for self-checking. Then place the cards in a resealable plastic bag and clip the bag of cards to the chart. Suspend each pocket chart from a skirt hanger. A student sorts each bag of cards into the pockets of the corresponding chart. The skirt hanger allows the child to easily turn the chart from side to side.

JoAnn Giammalva—Gr. 1
Millsap Elementary, Cypress, TX

Book Wheels

For a fun alternative to book reports, have students complete book wheels. At a center, place scissors, crayons, pencils, brads, and a supply of construction-paper wheels and wheel covers. To make a book wheel, a student sequentially numbers the sections of a wheel from one to eight. Then, working in sequential order, he describes and illustrates eight events from the book he read. On the wheel cover he writes the title and author of the book and completes an illustration if desired. Then, using a brad, he attaches the wheel cover atop the wheel. Presto! He's ready to take a spin with reading.

Debbie Grecco—Gr. 3
Northwest School, Butler, PA

Photo Album Fun

Make descriptive writing a personal matter with this writing activity. Have each youngster bring a photograph from home that can be included in a class photo album. At a center, place a photo album containing a supply of 8 1/2" x 11" self-adhesive pages and a supply of writing paper. Also post a list of questions such as the ones shown. Using the posted questions as a guide, a student writes a descriptive paragraph about his snapshot. Then he attaches the photograph and his paragraph to a blank album page. When each student has completed the center, place the album in your classroom library for all to enjoy.

Rachelle Dawson—Gr. 3
Nashua School, Kansas City, MO

WHO is in the picture?
WHERE was the picture taken?
WHAT was happening in the picture?
WHEN was the picture taken?
WHY did you choose to bring this picture to school?

My dog Sofie loves to eat. Here she is begging at a picnic we had last summer. I think she is sweet.

CREATIVE WRITING

Pick A Pet

Your animal lovers will find this center especially appealing. From discarded magazines, cut an assortment of animal pictures. Place the cutouts and a supply of writing and construction paper at a center. After choosing a picture, a student writes a paragraph in which he describes the animal and explains why it would make a terrific pet. Then he mounts the picture and his paragraph on construction paper, and trims the construction paper to create an eye-catching border. Display the completed projects on a bulletin board titled "Pick A Pet."

Adapted from an idea by
Leigh Anne Newsom—Gr. 3
Greenbrier Intermediate
Chesapeake, VA

This dog loves to snorkel. It will swim right next to you. It can even fetch shells underwater. This dog would be fun to have as a pet.

Snapshot Stories

Reading comprehension practice becomes a snap for students at this center! Keep a camera handy for taking candid snapshots of your students engaged in a variety of activities. Mount and number selected snapshots on the inside of a file folder. Write a simple sentence caption for each picture on a 4 1/2" x 2" card. Program the backs of the cards for self-checking; then laminate if desired. Place cards in a Press-On Pocket attached to the back of the folder. The student reads and places the captions under the appropriate pictures, then flips the cards to check. Next have the student write a story about the events shown in the pictures. Start a collection of snapshot stories today!

Nadine Docherty and Gaylona Kline—
Special Education
Anna Jarvis Elementary School
Grafton, WV

A Friendly Letter

Attract student interest at this center by using magnetic media! Indicate the five parts of a friendly letter on a sheet of poster board; then attach a magnet to each part as shown. Next label individual cards with the names of the letter parts and attach a magnet to the back of each card. Students match the cards to the poster, then check their work against a provided answer key. To extend the activity, have each student write a friendly letter to a real or imaginary friend on provided writing paper.

Reba S. Walden—Chapter 1
Granite Falls Elementary School
Granite Falls, NC

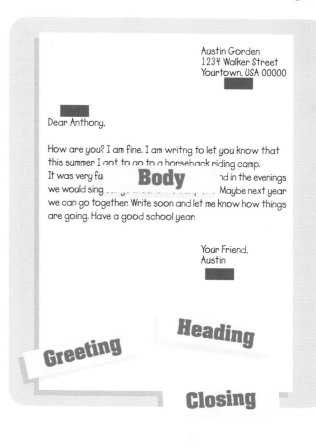

Austin Gorden
1234 Walker Street
Yourtown, USA 00000

Dear Anthony,

How are you? I am fine. I am writng to let you know that this summer I got to go to a horseback riding camp. It was very fu_____ nd in the evenings we would sing _____. Maybe next year we can go together. Write soon and let me know how things are going. Have a good school year.

Your Friend,
Austin

Greeting **Heading**

Body

Closing

I saw a baby bird in a bird's nest!

Gerry 3-26-96

Do You See What I See?

Sharpen your youngsters' observation skills at this year-round center. Near a window place a pair of binoculars, a booklet with blank pages, and a supply of pencils, markers, and crayons. A student uses the binoculars to look closely at objects outside the window. Then he writes and/or illustrates an account of what he saw on a blank booklet page. When the pages of the booklet are filled, title and date the booklet before displaying it in your reading corner. Then place another booklet of blank pages at the center.

Lisa Tonkery—Gr. 1
Avon Elementary
Grayslake, IL

CREATIVE WRITING

Picture-Perfect Ideas

If you're a classroom shutterbug, here's an easy way to provide your budding authors with loads of writing inspiration! Each time you develop a roll of school-related snapshots, request double prints. Mat your extra set of prints on individual pieces of colorful construction paper; then exhibit five or six photos from the set at a center. (Save the rest of the matted photos for later use.) Supply the center with writing paper, designer pencils, and a children's dictionary. Students can write stories about their favorite snapshots or create individual captions for the collection. Keep writing interest high by routinely replacing the photos with yet-to-be-seen snapshots from your ongoing collection. Write on!

Natalie R. Johnson—Gr. 2
Edison Elementary
Lawton, OK

Shapely Stories

Student writing takes shape with these individual booklets. Laminate six 4 1/2" x 6" construction-paper rectangles. Using an X-acto® knife, cut the same shape from each rectangle. Sort the cutouts and the resulting stencils into two piles. To make a word bank, program each cutout with a word related to its shape; then use a metal ring to fasten the cutouts together. Place the word bank, the stencils, a supply of 4 1/2" x 6" writing paper and construction paper, a stapler, scissors, pencils, and markers or crayons at a center. To make a five-page booklet, a student uses a stencil to trace the booklet shape onto five pieces of writing paper and two pieces of construction paper. Next he cuts out the shapes and staples the pages between the covers. Then, using the word bank, he writes a story in his booklet. When he is finished writing, the student illustrates his story and booklet cover as desired. By varying the shape and size, you can create a multitude of booklet possibilities.

Susie J. Gresham
Thornton, AR

Add An Ending

Put your old children's magazines to good use. Cut out interesting stories from the magazines, omitting the endings or other important parts. Glue each story inside a folder. Add words with which students can finish the story. Place the folders in a box. The student selects a folder, reads the story, and writes his own ending. Let students share their new stories with the rest of the class.

Marilyn Borden—Gr. 3
Castleton Elementary School
Bomoseen, VT

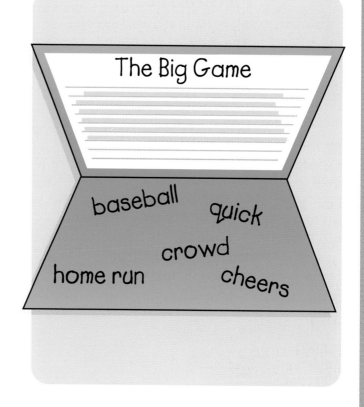

Paragraphs, Please!

Encourage students to write good paragraphs using longer and more complex sentence forms. Make activity cards that feature small, interesting pictures. Describe the picture with four short, repetitive sentences. Provide students with pencil-shaped booklets with enough lined pages to complete all of the activity cards. Encourage children to indent the paragraphs, join the sentences together, and add at least two ideas of their own.

Beth Jones
General Vanier School
Niagara Falls, Ontario
Canada

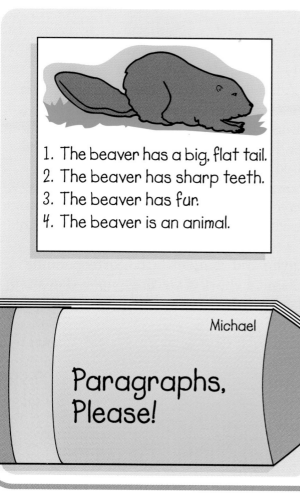

1. The beaver has a big, flat tail.
2. The beaver has sharp teeth.
3. The beaver has fur.
4. The beaver is an animal.

Michael

Paragraphs, Please!

CREATIVE WRITING

Picture This!

Provide great writing motivation and put an end to the often-repeated phrase, "I don't know what to write about!" with this easy-to-make center. Keep a camera close at hand and snap candid photographs of special classroom and school activities. Enlarge the camera pattern on page 80. Color, cut out, and glue the camera to the front of a file folder. Inside the folder draw a picture frame slightly larger than your photograph and write student directions and guidelines. Laminate the folder; then tape a photograph inside the frame. When desired, just replace the existing photograph and you have a brand-new writing center!

Kathy Quinlan—Gr. 1
Lithia Springs Elementary
Lithia Springs, GA

Did you tell...
—what is happening?
—when it happened?
—where it happened?
—how it happened?

Now check your story for...
✓ spelling
✓ capital letters
✓ punctuation
✓ your name

Colorful Creations

Add a touch of color to your writing center! Duplicate the crayon patterns on page 81 onto several colors of construction paper. Program each crayon with a color-related writing activity (such as the ones shown); then laminate and cut out the crayons. Display the crayon cutouts in a discarded crayon box along with a supply of writing paper. A student chooses a crayon and completes the corresponding task on a sheet of writing paper. If desired, also provide crayons and a supply of construction paper at the center. A student can decorate his work and then mount it atop a sheet of matching construction paper.

Shelley Clayburn—Resource
Clinton Elementary
Lincoln, NE

List six things that make you feel blue.

List ten yellow things.

List ten words that rhyme with *red*.

red

1. bed
2. said
3. lead
4. fed
5. dead
6. sled
7. wed
8. head
9. Fred
10. Ned

Mini-Math

Prepare a week's worth of math-fact practice in an instant! Write "Mini-Math" at the top of a tagboard strip and laminate. Write in an operation, followed by a list of ten numbers, with a wipe-off marker. Students visit the center and record their answers in mini-math booklets. Each day, change only the operation on the strip to create ten new problems. At the end of the week, wipe the strip clean and reprogram. Provide supplies for booklet construction at the center each Monday. (Materials needed per child: five 2" x 8 1/2" paper strips, two 3" x 9" construction-paper strips for covers, and a stapler.)

Beth Jones
General Vanier School
Niagara Falls, Ontario
Canada

M
I
N
I
M
A
T
H

Mini-Math
+9

16

24

31

53

60

72

95

28

49

87

Filled To The Brim

Create a thirst for math-fact practice at this matching center. To make each activity, stack two Styrofoam® cups. Label the outside cup with a series of math facts; then label the rim of the inside cup with the corresponding answers. (See the illustration.) Unstack the cups and store them at a center. To complete the center, a student restacks the cups so that the facts and answers correspond. Supply an answer key for self-checking. To increase the difficulty of the center, program the outer cups so that fact answers appear more than once.

Jane Kjosen—Learning Disabilities
Jefferson Elementary
Fargo, ND

Trimming The Tree

Put a twinkle in math-fact practice this holiday season! For a gameboard, enlarge the tree shape on page 82 onto poster board. From several colors of construction paper, cut 20 tree-light shapes. The light cutouts must be the same size as those on the gameboard. Attach a folded black paper strip (cut with pinking shears) to the top of each light cutout. Program each cutout with a math-fact problem; then program the gameboard with the corresponding answers. Laminate all pieces for durability. Place the gameboard, the cutouts (in a resealable plastic bag), and copies of page 82 at the center. A student first matches the cutouts to the gameboard, then colors a worksheet so it corresponds to the gameboard.

Annette Roybal—Gr. 2
Monte Vista Elementary
Monte Vista, CO

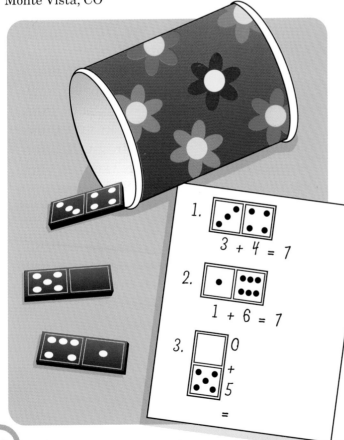

Domino Sums

This math center adds up to lots of fun. Store a desired number of dominoes in a decorated container. Place the container and a supply of blank paper at a center. A student removes a domino from the container and sketches its likeness on his paper. Below or beside his drawing, he writes and solves the addition problem that corresponds to the domino dot pattern. To check his work, he counts the total number of dots on the domino. The student continues in this manner until he has calculated a sum for each domino in the container. Challenge older students to create and solve a subtraction and/or multiplication fact that corresponds to each domino dot pattern.

Suzanne Walz—Gr. 1
West Wendover Elementary
Wendover, NV

Slip-sliding Slalom

Take the chill out of basic math-fact practice with this "slick" sorting poster. Enlarge the pattern on page 83 onto poster board. At the same time, make a matching flag pattern from the enlargement to use for making fact cards. Cut out and label fact cards with correct and incorrect math facts. Or program cards with correctly or incorrectly spelled words. Color-code the backs of flags for self-checking if desired.

Mathematically Inclined Cereal

Use Kellogg's two-toned cereal, Crispix®, as a manipulative when teaching number combinations. Have each child toss some Crispix® out of a cup. Then have her write the corresponding addition equation to show how many yellow and brown sides are exposed. For subtraction practice, have students record the total number of Crispix® and subtract the number of brown ones from the total.

Julie Mitchell
Wilt Elementary School
Louisville, KY

BASIC MATH SKILLS

It's A Match!

Keep your youngsters mathematically challenged at this matching center. On each of several 2" x 6" tagboard strips, use a marker to write a vertical math fact. Space the numerals evenly and omit the line above the answer. To make the cards self-checking, code the backs of the cards as shown. Laminate the cards for durability; then cut each strip into three pieces by cutting between the numerals. Store the cutouts in a decorative container at the center. A student removes the cards, reassembles the facts, and checks his work by turning over the cards.

You can easily design several sets of cards to meet the mathematical needs of your youngsters. For identification purposes, color-code the sets by using different colors of tagboard strips. Students just learning their facts need only a few cards to keep them challenged. For those students who have extraordinary math skills, consider combining two or three math operations in one card set.

Bernice C. White—Gr. 1
St. Joseph School
Sharon, PA

Just Like Magic!

If you're running short on center space, try this magnetic center approach. Attach a colorful border cut from Con-Tact® paper around the perimeter of one side of your file cabinet. Create a manipulative center such as the one shown; then attach a small square of Magnetic Tape (available from The Education Center, Inc.) to the back of each center piece. Students complete the center by manipulating the pieces on the surface of the file cabinet. It works like magic! (See patterns on pages 84 and 85.)

Marilyn Borden—Gr. 3
Castleton Elementary School
Bomoseen, VT

Spider Math

Here's a creepy, crawly, fun way to practice math skills! Duplicate several copies of the spider pattern on page 86 on construction paper. Label each spider body with a sum. Write matching number sentences on the legs. Have children find the matching legs for each spider body. Color-code the backs of the pieces for self-checking. Make more of these spooky spiders for practicing subtraction and multiplication facts, too.

Sandra Burns Workman
Taylors, SC

Getting To The Core!

Provide students with a healthy portion of basic fact practice at this math center. Duplicate fruit shapes (patterns on pages 87–89). Program one half of the cutout with an answer; then program the other half of the cutout with a corresponding math fact. Cut each cutout into two pieces (using a variety of cutting patterns). For durability, laminate all pieces; then store pieces in a Ziploc® bag. Students place the corresponding facts and answers together. If the two pieces fit together, a student knows he has matched them correctly.

Viola Gardner
Bertrand, NE

BASIC MATH SKILLS

Fill 'er Up!

Sorting even and odd numbers means big business at this math center. Using the patterns on page 90 and colorful construction paper, duplicate two gas pumps and a supply of cars. Label one gas pump "even" and the other pump "odd"; then program the cars with even and odd numbers. Laminate and cut out the patterns. Using a permanent marker, program the back of each car cutout for self-checking. Store all of the cutouts in a Ziploc® bag at a center. A student steers each car to the correct gas pump, then flips the cutout to check his work. Fill 'er up!

Joanne Spuches—Gr. 1
Birch Wathen Lenox
New York, NY

Seasonal Calculations

Watch your youngsters' math facts take shape at this seasonal center. Trace a supply of seasonal shapes on construction paper. Use the hole-punched strips from computer paper to create a set on each shape. Laminate and cut out the shapes; then store them in a gift-wrapped box like the one shown. Place the box and a supply of paper at a center. A student removes two cutouts from the box, then writes and solves the corresponding addition (or subtraction or multiplication) fact on his paper. He then returns the shapes to the box and removes two more. He continues in this manner until he has completed a predetermined number of math facts.

For a fun partner game, have each student remove one cutout from the box and place it faceup on the playing area. The first student to declare the correct sum, difference, or product of the cutouts wins them. Play continues in this manner until all of the cutouts have been won. The player with the most cutouts at the end of the game wins.

adapted from an idea by Mary Cibulsky
Chapter I Resource Room Teaching Assistant
Sabal Elementary, Melbourne, FL

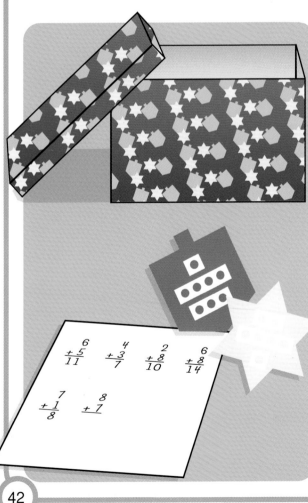

Pigskin Countdown

If counting to 100 is a goal for your team, try this game plan. To make the gameboard, use white paint to visually divide a sheet of green poster board into 11 equal sections. Laminate. Using a permanent marker, label the sections for counting practice. Beginning with zero, allow for ten numerals per section (approximately two inches per numeral), but program only three. Label the final section with the numeral 100. Attach a piece of self-adhesive Velcro® to the gameboard to represent each missing numeral. Next label 70 laminated football cutouts with the missing numerals. Attach Velcro® to the backs of the cutouts. Store the cutouts in a football helmet. A student places each football cutout in its correct position on the gridiron gameboard.

Easy Does It!

When you need a learning center at a moment's notice, this sorting center is the perfect solution. Using a marker and pieces of masking tape, label each section of a muffin tin to correspond with a desired sorting skill. Then place the tin and a basket of objects (for sorting) at the center. Suggestions include:

- Label each section with numerals or number words. Supply the exact number of counters needed.
- Label each section with a color word. Provide an assortment of appropriately colored buttons.
- Label each section with an amount of money. Supply the correct coins needed to make each amount.

Susan Voss—Gr. 1
Knapp School

43

COUNTING

Spin And Count

Give counting practice an exciting twist with this partner activity! Duplicate four copies of a hundreds chart (page 91). Set aside one chart to be used for regular counting practice. Then use markers to program the remaining three charts for counting by twos, threes, and fives. Laminate all four charts. Store the charts in a box lid at a center. Also provide a toy top.

To begin the activity, one student removes the counting charts from the box lid. Then, in turn, each youngster places one chart in the box lid, sets the toy top in the center of the chart, and spins the top. When the top stops spinning, the student that spun the top begins counting to 100—starting with the number under the top. The partner refers to the counting chart to assist and monitor the student who is counting. The youngsters continue in this manner until each one has spun the top four times (once atop each chart) and completed each counting practice.

Phyllis Kidder—Gr. 1
Edward C. Killin Elementary School
Okinawa, Japan

Feed this pig.
Count by tens.

10 20 30 40

Pigging Out On Numbers

Youngsters can go hog-wild over this counting center! Using the patterns on page 92 and 93, duplicate four pigs onto pink construction paper and 50 ears of corn onto yellow construction paper. Number the ears of corn from 1 to 50. Then program each pig with a counting direction such as "Feed this pig. Count by fives," or "Feed this pig. Count by twos." Laminate and cut out the shapes; then attach a small square of magnetic tape to the back of each piece. Store the cutouts in a resealable plastic bag. A student attaches a pig to the surface of a file cabinet or a magnetic chalkboard; then she arranges the ears of corn to match. With a quick glance, you can check the child's work and give her immediate feedback.

Dolores Joiner—Gr. 1
Furry Elementary
Sandusky, OH

We Love To Estimate!

Better estimating skills are just a heart-beat away with this fun center activity! Cut a set of cards from red poster board. Draw a heart on each card, varying the sizes of the hearts. Place the cards at a center with a bag of heart-shaped valentine candies. A child chooses a card and estimates the number of candies needed to completely fill in the heart outline. After recording his estimate on his paper, the student actually covers the heart with candies, counting as he works. He then records his total and compares it with his estimate. How sweet it is!

Beth Jones
Niagara Falls, Ontario
Canada

Countable Collectables

Reinforce estimating and counting skills at this hands-on center. To begin, fill or partially fill each of ten baby food jars with a different item that is suitable for estimating and counting. Use masking tape and a marker to sequentially number the jars and indicate the jars' contents. (See the illustration.) Store the jars in a decorated shoebox. Place the box of jars and a supply of duplicated response sheets like the one shown at a center. A student chooses a jar and records its contents on his response sheet; then he estimates the number of items in the jar and records his estimate. Next he carefully removes the jar lid and counts the items. After recording his count, he replaces the items and the lid, and returns the jar to the box. Finally he evaluates his work and writes a related comment on his paper. The student repeats this procedure for each of the remaining jars. When all students have completed the center, simply empty the jars; then refill the jars as desired and relabel them accordingly. Place a new supply of response sheets in the center, and the center's ready to use again.

Lisa Desrosiers—Gr. K–3 Special Education
Harlow Street School
Worcester, MA

#2 COTTON BALLS

Name Zachary

Jar #1: pom-poms   Estimate: 25
                        Count: 22

Comment: I was really close!

Jar #2: cotton balls   Estimate: 12
                        Count:

Comment:

GRAPHING

Mighty Mouth!

There's no doubt that this graphing center will attract lots of student interest! Fill a container with magnetic items such as paper clips and paper fasteners. Place the container, a supply of duplicated graphs such as the one shown, and a Mighty Mouth puppet at a center. To make the puppet, attach two wiggle eyes, a pom-pom nose, and a magnet mouth to an adult-size sock. (See illustration.) A student slips his hand inside the puppet. Then, using his fingers to manipulate the puppet's mouth, he guides the puppet into the container and extracts a "mouthful" of magnetic items. Next he sorts and counts these items and records his information on a graph. He then returns the magnetic items to the container.

Bernice C. White—Gr. 1
St. Joseph School
Sharon, PA

Falling For Leaves

Just watch your students breeze through this independent graphing activity! Duplicate a student supply of the graph on page 94; then place the graphs and a basket of leaves at the center. A student chooses eight leaves from the basket and sorts them according to the categories shown on the graph. Next he colors the graph to show his findings. If desired, post a color-coded graph at the center for those students who are not yet reading color words.

Rochelle R. Slachta—Gr. 1
VanRaalte Elementary
Holland, MI

Pot O' Gold

Filling this pot with golden coins adds up to a great addition or multiplication practice. Provide a tagboard pot cutout (pattern on page 95) and program as shown. Store 17 golden circles (labeled with matching sums or products) in a pocket on the back of the cutout.

To play, a student adds or multiplies adjacent numbers, then places the corresponding "coin" in the circular space between them.

Linda Locklier—Compensatory Teacher
Fort Mill, SC

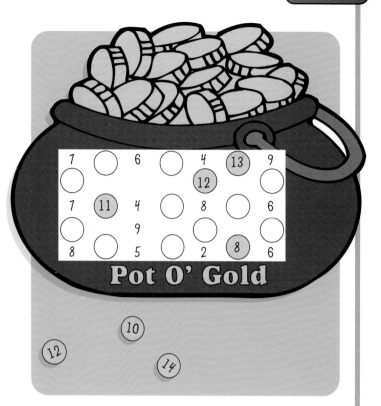

Shop Till You Drop!

Instant smiles will appear when students begin shopping for toys at this math center! Glue catalog pictures of toys to the inside of a file folder. Label pictures with prices appropriate for your students. Attach a library pocket to the outside of the file folder. Program index cards with activities for the students to complete inside the toy store. Place cards in the library pocket. Complete the folder by adding desired directions and decorations.

Carolyn Barwick
Madison Heights, MI

Ribbon Measurement

This colorful center can easily be tailored to meet your youngsters' measurement needs. Glue an assortment of premeasured ribbon lengths to the inside of a file folder. Number the ribbon lengths and add desired student directions. For self-checking, program the back of the folder with an answer key. Decorate the front of the folder as desired, then laminate the opened folder for durability. Refold the folder and place it in a center along with a ruler and a supply of paper. A student measures each of the ribbon lengths and records his answers on a sheet of paper. Then he checks his work using the answer key on the back of the folder. Since making this center is a snap, you can easily make a folder for each of several different units of measurement.

Kari Case—Gr. 1
Sanborn Christian School
Sanborn, IA

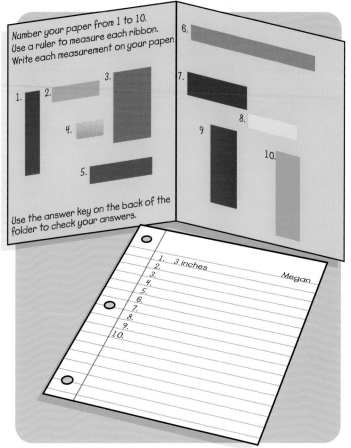

Number your paper from 1 to 10.
Use a ruler to measure each ribbon.
Write each measurement on your paper.

1. 2. 3.
4.
5.
6.
7.
8.
9.
10.

Use the answer key on the back of the folder to check your answers.

1. 3 inches
2.
3. Megan
4.
5.
6.
7.
8.
9.
10.

2 cups

4 cups

¾ cup

Macaroni Measurements

Students quickly discover how their math skills measure up at this hands-on center. Use Con-Tact® paper to cover a collection of different-sized containers. Label each container with a different measurement. Then, using measuring cups, measure the appropriate amount of elbow macaroni into each container. Next empty the contents of the containers into a large plastic bowl. Place the bowl of macaroni, the measuring cups, and the labeled containers at a center. A student uses the measuring cups to measure the appropriate amount of macaroni into each labeled container. If a student measures accurately, he will have exactly the right amount of macaroni!

Money Matters

At this center, students make "cents" of counting money. Decorate the lid of an egg carton as desired; then press a sticky dot that has been labeled with an alphabet letter into each egg cup. Next place a combination of coins (totaling less than one dollar) in each cup. Create a corresponding answer key; then place the egg carton, the answer key, a hundreds chart, and a supply of paper at the center. To determine the amount of money in each egg cup, a student removes the coins from a cup; then, beginning with the highest-value coin and working in descending order, he places the coins on the hundreds chart as shown. When the last coin has been placed, he writes the corresponding number of cents and the letter in the cup on his paper. When the student has completed the activity, he uses the answer key to check his work. (Patterns on pages 96 and 97.)

Gayle Vledder-Jones
Speech and Language

1	2	3	4	5	6	7	8	9	10
11	12	13	14	15	16	17	18	19	20
21	22	23	24		26	27	28	29	30
31	32	33	34			37	38	39	40
41	42	43	44	45	46	47	48	49	50
51	52	53	54	55	56	57	58	59	60
61	62	63	64	65	66	67	68	69	70
71	72	73	74	75	76	77	78	79	80
81	82	83	84	85	86	87	88	89	90
91	92	93	94	95	96	97	98	99	100

Handy Money Game

Encourage your students to go on a buying spree in this money-skills center. Using the coin patterns on pages 96 and 97, glue a set to each of ten hand-shaped cutouts. Provide 20 cards (two for each value on the hand cutouts) bearing pictures of items kids can "buy" with the coin combinations. Label each card with a price. Have the students take turns determining the value of a coin set, and matching an item of equal value that they wish to "purchase."

Judy Peterson

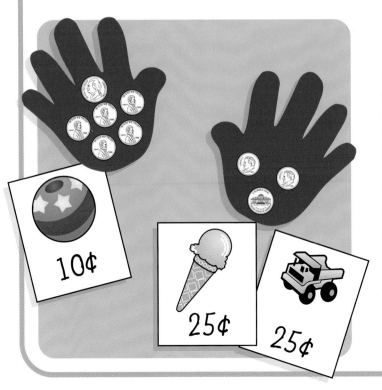

49

MONEY SKILLS

A Shower Of Money!

The forecast at this math center is money, money, money! Cut out a large poster-board umbrella and divide it into sections as shown. Laminate the umbrella. Using a wipe-off marker, write a money amount in each section. The student counts out and places a matching amount of coin cutouts on each section of the umbrella. Check student work or provide an answer key listing the possible coin combinations for each amount.

For an added challenge, program the umbrella for practice in making change. Write a money amount in the top section of the umbrella and lesser amounts in the remaining sections. The student places coin cutouts on each section to equal the change he would receive based on the top amount of money. (Patterns on pages 96 and 97.)

Robert Kinker
Bexley, OH

Cashing In On Coupons

If you're looking for a real deal to reinforce money skills, this math center is just what you need. Clip a supply of grocery store coupons from magazines and newspapers. Place the coupons at a center along with glue, a set of coin cutouts (patterns on pages 96 and 97), a ruler, a pencil, and a supply of 9" x 6" sheets of construction paper. A student glues a coupon near the top of his construction paper. Then, using the coin cutouts, he glues on several possible combinations that equal the value of the coupon. Instruct students to draw lines between the coin combinations as shown. Now that's a bargain!

Barbara Leach—Gr. 2
Parker School
Tolland, CT

Valentine Mail

All you need to sweeten money skills is a package of commercial valentines. Using the coin cutouts on pages 96 and 97, glue a coin amount on the back of each valentine. "Address" the envelopes with matching amounts. The student inserts each valentine inside its matching envelope. For self-checking, "hide" the correct amount somewhere on the front of each valentine. Store the valentines and envelopes in a valentine candy box or canister.

Everything's A Dollar!

Talk about value! Here's a center that takes a minimal amount of effort to create and it's one that students will visit time and time again! At a center, display a code that assigns a cent value to each alphabet letter. You will also need a calculator, a dictionary, a supply of scratch paper, pencils, pushpins, and duplicated dollar bills (pattern on page 98). Using the code, calculator, and dictionary, a student searches for words whose letters equal 100 cents. When he finds a word that has not already been discovered (discovered words are pinned near the code), he writes the word on a duplicated dollar bill (in the oval) and signs his name as the "Founder." Then he pins the bill near the code.

Each day enlist a Secretary Of The Treasury. At a designated time, this student checks the newly posted bills for accuracy. If the Secretary finds that a bill is accurate (the word is spelled correctly and the value of the letters equals 100 cents), he signs the bill on the provided line and redisplays it at the center. If the Secretary finds an error, he returns the bill to its founder. Reward each founder of a "legal" bill with a gold-wrapped chocolate coin. If desired, give your Secretary Of The Treasury an edible coin for his efforts.

Diana Vrooman—Gr. 3

MULTIPLICATION FACTS

Ticklish Toes

Your students will be tickled to practice their math at the Ticklish Toes Center! After cutting two large foot shapes, write a different number on each toe. Cut 12 feather shapes, labeling each with an identifying letter to aid in correction. Write math problems on the feathers and laminate. Children choose a feather and use the numbers on the toes to write problems in foot-shaped booklets. (Patterns on page 99.)

Beth Jones
General Vanier School
Fort Erie, Ontario
Canada

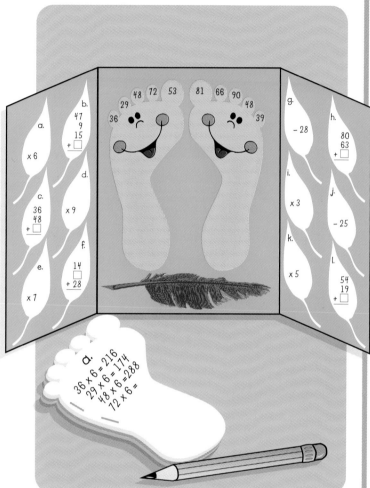

Pull the strip up.
Write the problem and answer.

Boo Juice

Spread Halloween cheer with this tachistoscope activity. Use poster board to make a cutout like the one shown. Then provide several programmed strips for math-fact practice. Write the answer below each problem for self-checking. To complete this center, students write and solve each problem on their papers. (Pattern on page 100.)

Catalog Shopping

For this center enlist the help of your youngsters, family members, teaching colleagues, and friends in collecting an assortment of catalogs appropriate for classroom use. Attach a 9" x 12" Press-On Pocket to the back of each catalog, then store photocopies of the catalog's order form inside. A child studies a catalog and selects a predetermined number of items to order, then fills out an order form as if he were ordering the merchandise. Next he asks a classmate to review his work. When the twosome agree that his order form is completed satisfactorily, he turns it in. Because this center can be time-consuming to check, you may wish to enlist upper-grade students to help you.

Lee Henschel—Chapter I
Cypress Elementary
Pompano Beach, FL

Tally The Tapes

Cash in on easy-to-make math center activities by using cash register receipts. Number several receipts of assorted lengths. Next program task cards with math activities related to the receipts. Activities might include measuring the receipts to the nearest inch or centimeter, finding the sum of designated receipts, or counting out the amount of play money needed to make the purchase indicated on each receipt. Program the back of each card for self-checking and laminate the receipts and cards for durability, if desired. Store the receipts in a gift bag and the cards in a decorated box. Place the bag, box, and other needed materials at the center.

Diane Vogel—Grs. 2–3
W. B. Redding School
Macon, GA

Activity 1

Find the sum of tape 1 and tape 2.

SEQUENCING

Fine-feathered Sequencing

Students gobble up an assortment of sequencing skills at this center! Label several sets of colorful construction-paper feathers for sequencing practice. Label the backs of the feathers for self-checking; then use a brad to attach each set of feathers to a paper plate that has been painted brown. Attach a decorated turkey face and a pair of turkey feet to each plate. A student arranges each turkey's feathers in sequential order, then flips the turkeys to check his work. Gobble! Gobble!

Carole Shelby—Gr. 1
Ripley, MS

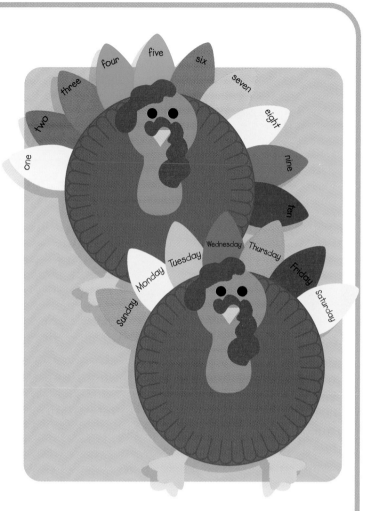

Happy Birthday To You!

Enlist your youngsters' help in creating this calendar sequencing activity. On white construction paper, duplicate student copies of the cupcake patterns on page 101. After each youngster has colored a cupcake, label his project with his name and birth date. Laminate and cut out the shapes; then use a permanent marker to program the backs of the cutouts for self-checking. Store the cutouts in a birthday gift bag. A student arranges the cutouts in sequential order; then he flips the cutouts to check his work. Happy birthday!

adapted from an idea by Sue Fichter—Gr. 2
St. Mary School
Des Plaines, IL

Countable Caterpillars

Not one youngster will try to wiggle out of doing this center! Remove the lids and thoroughly clean several plastic pill containers. Then place the containers, an ink pad, pencils, crayons, and drawing paper at a center. Add one or more task cards programmed with counting instructions. To make a caterpillar, a student inks the open end of a pill container and stamps a series of adjoining circles on his paper. Reinking the container as needed, he continues stamping circles until his caterpillar is the desired length. After decorating the caterpillar's head, the student sequentially numbers the remaining body sections as described on a task card. He completes his project by coloring a scene around his countable critter.

For practice alphabetizing, program a new task card with a list of letters or words. After a student creates his caterpillar, he uses the programming on the task card to alphabetically label its body.

Make a caterpillar with ten or more body sections.

Count by 2's.

Betsy Crosson—Gr. 1
Pleasant Elementary School
Tulare, CA

| January | February | March | April | May | June | July | August | September | October | November | December |

Giant Sequencing Puzzle

Make a large, durable puzzle to help students sequence the months of the year. Cut a 24" x 6" piece of wood (1/4" thick). With a jigsaw, cut the piece of wood into 12 pieces, using crooked lines. Paint each section a different color; then use permanent markers to decorate and label it with the name of a month. If desired, use poster board instead of wood, remembering to decorate and laminate the entire strip before cutting apart the sections.

Brenda Hancock—Gr. 1
Columbus, GA

TELLING TIME

Pocket Watch Practice

Add a little character to time-telling practice using old-time pocket watches. On tagboard, duplicate an equal number of pocket watch and pocket patterns (page 102). Laminate and cut out the patterns. Using a permanent marker, draw hands on the watch cutouts to represent times appropriate for your youngsters' skill levels. For each watch, program a pocket cutout with a matching digital time. For self-checking, put identical stickers on each matching pair. (Place the stickers on the fronts of the pockets and on the backs of the watches.) Glue the pockets inside a colorful folder. Store the watches in a Press-on Pocket attached to the back of the folder. To practice his time-telling skills, a youngster slips each watch into its matching pocket. My, how time flies when you're having fun practicing!

Karen Mount—Gr. 2
Canandaigua Primary School
Canandaigua, NY

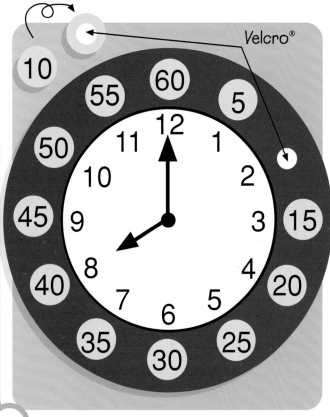

Velcro® Time-Telling

Students will think telling-time in five-minute intervals is "cinchy" with this class-size clock! Draw a large clock face on poster paper. Cut out, leaving a wide border. Using a contrasting color, cut out 12 construction-paper circles. Number the circles by fives to 60. Attach Velcro® to the circle backs. In the clock border next to the hour numbers, glue Velcro® dots. Fasten the numbered circles in place and the clock is ready to use. Or remove the circles from the clock, and have students replace them in their correct positions.

Dartha J. Williamson
North Jackson Elementary School
Athens, GA

Artistic Transformations

Foster students' creative thinking and artistic talents with this one-of-a-kind center! Each month draw or trace the outline of a seasonal shape on a blank sheet of paper; then duplicate student copies of the page on construction paper. Place the student papers and a supply of crayons, markers, or colored pencils at a center. A student transforms the seasonal shape into a totally unrelated object; then he illustrates a coordinating scene around the new object. Wow! Check this out!

Candy Whelan—Gr. 3
Carlough Elementary
St. Paul, MN

Notable Mosaics

Recycle construction-paper scraps at this versatile center. Enlarge the note pattern on page 103 to a desired size; then duplicate student copies on white construction paper. Place the copies, scissors, glue, a hole puncher, and a supply of construction-paper scraps at a center. A student cuts out a note; then she snips and punches a collection of colorful construction-paper scraps. Next she glues the pieces atop her note cutout until it is filled with colorful clippings. Every few weeks provide another duplicated shape for students to cut out and complete in the described manner.

Diana Leibbrandt—Gr. 1
Imperial Grade School
Imperial, NE

ART

Adorable Reindeer

These adorable reindeer may go down in history right beside Rudolph! In advance have each student paint three craft sticks brown. When dry, store each student's painted sticks in a resealable plastic bag labeled with her name. Place the bags, glue, and one six-inch, red pipe cleaner; one red pom-pom; and two wiggle eyes per student at the center. A student assembles her reindeer as shown, then stores it in her labeled bag. If desired, have an adult volunteer hot-glue a loop of gold thread to the back of each project so that it can be suspended.

Cathy Woodward—Gr. 3
McKinley Elementary
Newton, KS

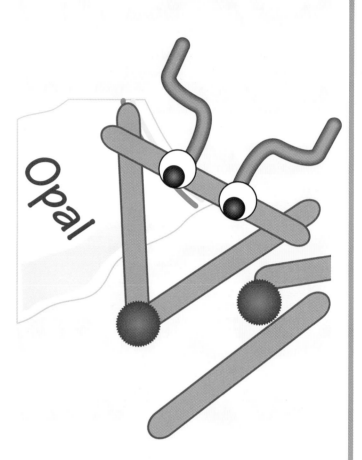

Creative Recycling

Here's a great way to inspire creativity and promote recycling. Have students create original greeting cards using folded 9" x 12" sheets of construction paper, an assortment of previously used cards, and a variety of arts-and-crafts supplies (such as gift wrap, wallpaper, and construction paper scraps; glitter; and markers). Students can design all-occasion cards or cards for specific celebrations, then present them to their family members or friends. When you care enough, you make it yourself!

Suzanne Edmunds
Forest Elementary
Forest, VA

Look At Frosty!

Beat the January blues with this just-for-fun art center. Place white chalk, scissors, glue, and a supply of construction-paper scraps at a center. You will also need a 12" x 18" sheet of dark-blue construction paper and three white doilies—incrementally sized—for each student. (To spare the expense of doilies, precut a supply of white paper squares in three incremental sizes. Have students cut snowflakes from the paper.) Students use the materials at the center to create personal renditions of Frosty. "Thumpity, thump, thump!"

Carolyn Hill—Gr. 2
Richland Elementary
Richland, MI

Me Booklets

Your youngsters won't be able to pass up this unique booklet-making opportunity. In advance make a blank booklet for each student. To do this bind together six 4 1/2" x 9" strips of tagboard. (See the illustration.) Place the booklets at a center along with crayons, markers, scissors, glue, and four 4 1/2" x 9" strips of tagboard per student.

To create a "Me!" booklet, a student chooses a blank booklet and four tagboard strips. On each strip he draws and colors a large picture, then cuts it out. One picture must be a likeness of himself. The remaining pictures may be people and/or objects that he likes. After designing his booklet cover, he glues one cutout to each booklet page so that the figures extend above the booklet pages. He then adds desired captions and decorations to the pages and the back cover. Spectacular!

Jane Rees
Westside School
Herrin, IL

ART

Copycat Center

Reassure your students that it's okay to copy at this center! Mount a coloring book picture onto a sheet of colored construction paper and laminate. Display the picture at the center. Students attempt to redraw the picture onto their papers, then color their drawings.

Rebecca Gibson Calton
Auburn, AL

'Tis Time To Draw!

Your amateur artists will get a kick out of this versatile drawing activity. Duplicate the gameboard on page 104 and place several copies in a center along with pencils, game pawns, and a die.

To play, students take turns rolling a die and moving the corresponding number of spaces on their gameboards. Upon landing on a space, the student draws that part of Mr. Potato on the incomplete potato on his gameboard. (If he lands on a part he does not need, he loses his turn.) The first player to complete his Mr. Potato picture wins.

Program and duplicate other seasonal gameboards: spring—chick, Halloween—jack-o'-lantern, Thanksgiving—pilgrim, or Christmas—Santa.

Loretta Lyon
Derby Hills Elementary School
Derby, KS

Cereal Creations

Challenge students to hop on the cereal bandwagon and create an array of new cereal products for health-conscious consumers. After deciding on a new cereal creation, the student designs a full-page advertisement which includes the name and a drawing of the product, the ingredients in the product, and a short paragraph explaining why this cereal is better than any other health cereal on the market. Have students contribute empty cereal boxes to the center; then redecorate the boxes to represent their new products. Display student work at the center.

HONEY BEES!

Ingredients: honey, oat flour, molasses

Transportation Trendsetter

Put youngsters' creative and productive thinking skills in gear at this transportation center. Stock the center with a large box filled with an assortment of throwaway items (such as plastic bottles, toilet tissue rolls, bottle caps, plastic lids, buttons, straws, etc.), glue, tape, and string. A student uses the materials in the center to create an original form of transportation. Label each child's creation with his name and the name of his vehicle; then add it to a classroom display. Vrrroom!

Mary Begley
St. Charles Primary
Chippewa Falls, WI

SS Jeff

Jeff's Submarine

Crayon Corner

Add a splash of color to skill review! Using the patterns on page 81, duplicate a colorful assortment of construction-paper crayons. Label each crayon shape with a task associated with a large box of crayons such as "Find four crayons that begin with the blend *bl*," and "Choose six crayons. Write the names of the crayon colors in alphabetical order." Laminate the programmed shapes for durability and cut them out. Store the crayon cutouts, a large box of crayons, a ruler, a supply of paper, and other needed supplies at a center. A student chooses a predetermined number of colorful tasks to complete.

Diane Fortunato—Gr. 2
Carteret School
Bloomfield, NJ

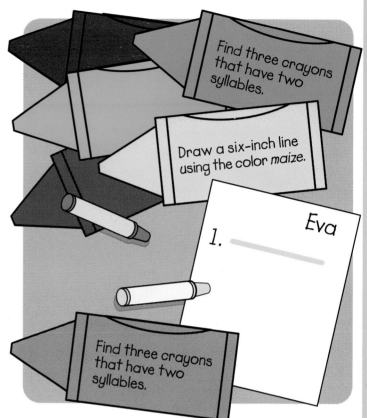

Patterns

©1996 The Education Center, Inc.

Bunny Business

Disguised as a bunny, this center will be difficult to keep a lid on. Use the patterns to prepare several construction-paper bunny and tail cutouts. Program the bunnies and tails for matching skills such as: antonyms, synonyms, homonyms, words/abbreviations, Arabic numerals/Roman numerals, basic math facts/answers. Store the pieces in a large can decorated to resemble a bunny.

Students match the bunnies to the corresponding tails for bunches of basic skills practice.

Elizabeth Harris—ESL Teacher
Kimball Elementary School
Mesquite, TX

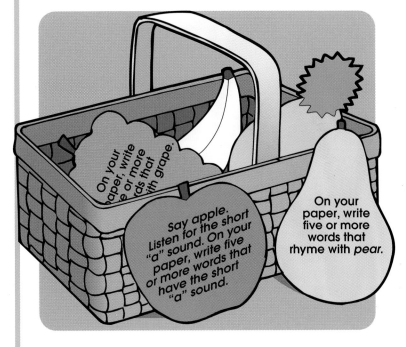

A Basketful Of Fruit

Create a basketful of skill review at this "a-peeling" center! Using the patterns on page 105, enlarge and duplicate each fruit shape onto the appropriate color of construction paper. Program each shape with a review activity. For added fun, relate the activities to the fruit shapes. (See the programmed samples.) Add desired details with markers; then laminate shapes for durability and cut them out. Place the cutouts in a basket. Then display the basket, paper, pencils, crayons or markers, and other needed supplies at the center.

adapted from an idea by Kathleen Darby—Gr. 1
Community School
Cumberland, RI

Try Some Brew!

Beware! Students may go batty at this high-interest multidisciplinary center! Program the inside of each of 12 folders with a task such as a creative-writing, following-directions, math, or reading activity. Number and attach a bubbling cauldron cutout to the front of each folder; then laminate. Place the folders in a decorated box and display at the center as shown using the witch pattern on page 106. Duplicate student copies of the management chart on page 107. Each time a student completes an activity, he colors the corresponding picture on his management chart. Reward students who complete a predetermined number of activities with a small prize, a tasty treat, or a special privilege. (Reward pattern on page 108.)

Cindy Fischer—Gr. 1
St. Mary's Grade School
Bismarck, ND

Magic Wand Activity Folders

When creating individual activity folders, consider this magnetic approach to self-checking. For each folder, you will need one folder and half of another file folder. Decorate the front of the folder as desired. Write the activities on the separate folder half, as shown, using multiple-choice answers. Attach a self-adhesive magnet behind each correct answer; then glue the half-folder inside the whole folder. Attach a self-adhesive magnet to a tongue depressor. Presto! A magic wand! Connect the wand to the folder with a piece of yarn. A correct answer is indicated by the attraction of two magnets. Magnetically attract students to any skill you choose!

Terriann P. Bonfini—Reading Specialist
Middle Creek Elementary
Wheeling, WV

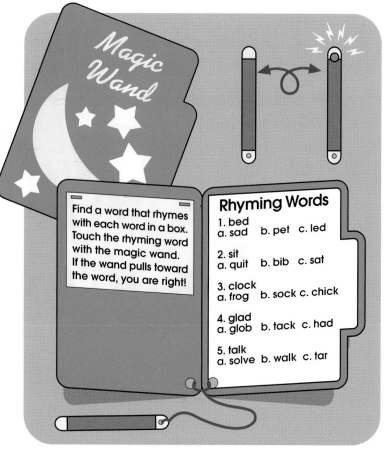

Magic Wand

Find a word that rhymes with each word in a box. Touch the rhyming word with the magic wand. If the wand pulls toward the word, you are right!

Rhyming Words

1. bed
   a. sad   b. pet   c. led

2. sit
   a. quit   b. bib   c. sat

3. clock
   a. frog   b. sock   c. chick

4. glad
   a. glob   b. tack   c. had

5. talk
   a. solve   b. walk   c. tar

Directions

funny

silly

Big Top Fun

Step right up! To make this circus-tent learning center, decorate each side of a large box to resemble a circus tent. To make the "top" of the tent, cut a large circle from heavy paper. Cut from the outside edge to the center of the circle; then fold the cutout into five equal sections. Unfold. Glue the first section atop the fifth section. If desired, scallop the edge of the resulting tent top before resting it atop the box. Attach a Press-On Pocket to each side of the tent. Using the patterns on pages 109 and 110, create four learning center activities. Place one activity on each side of the tent. Let the show begin!

Corina Ryland
Manhattan, KS

Patterns
Use with "The Stockings Were Hung"
on page 9.

Braille Alphabet

A B C D E F G H I J

K L M N O P Q R S T

U V W X Y Z and for of the

with ch sh th wh ed er ou ow ing

©1996 The Education Center, Inc. • *The Best Of The Mailbox® Learning Centers Primary* • TEC1455

Note To The Teacher: Use with "Happy Birthday, Mr. Braille" on page 10.

Patterns
Use with
"Jack-O'-Lantern
Contractions"
on page 12.

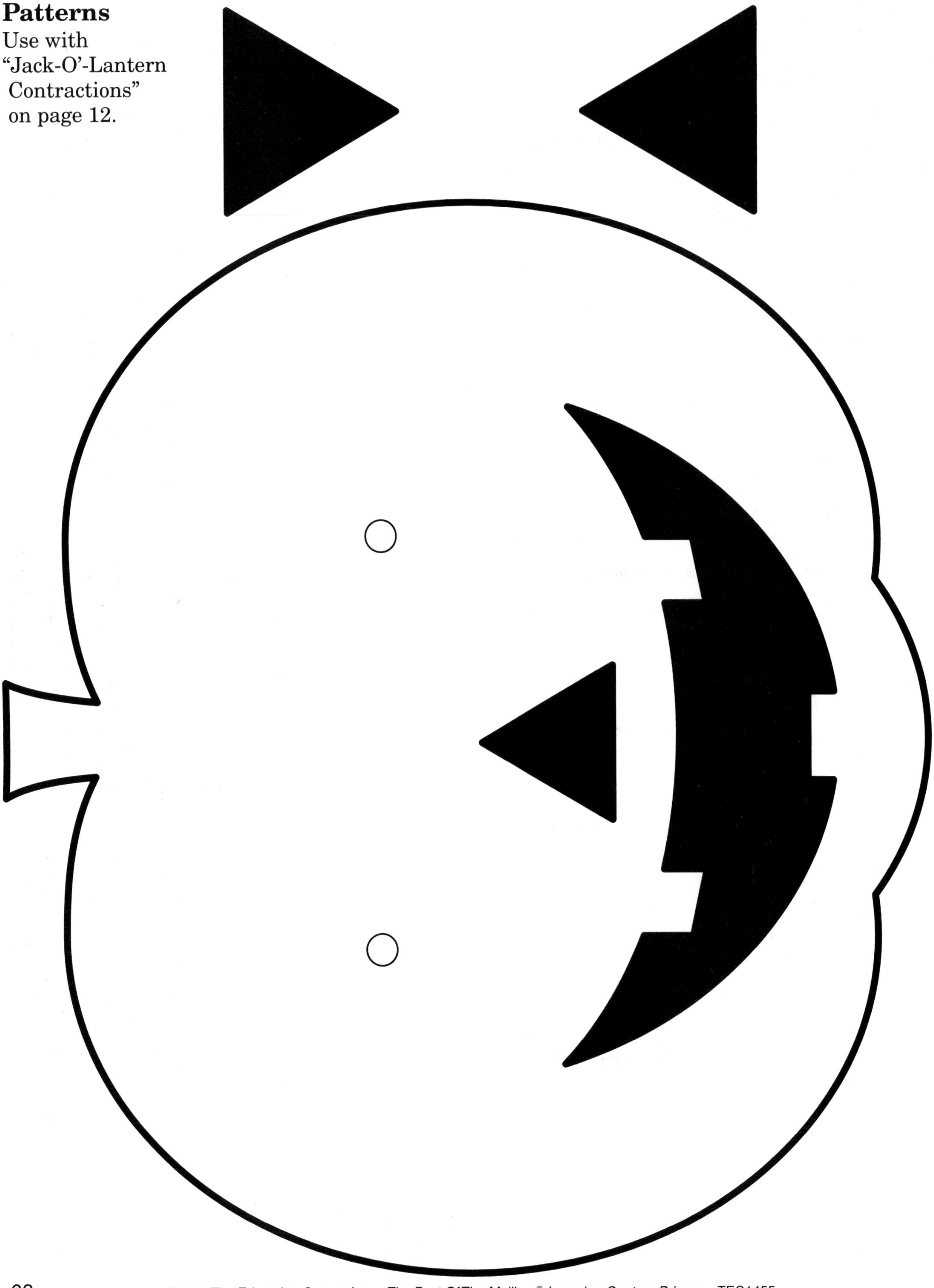

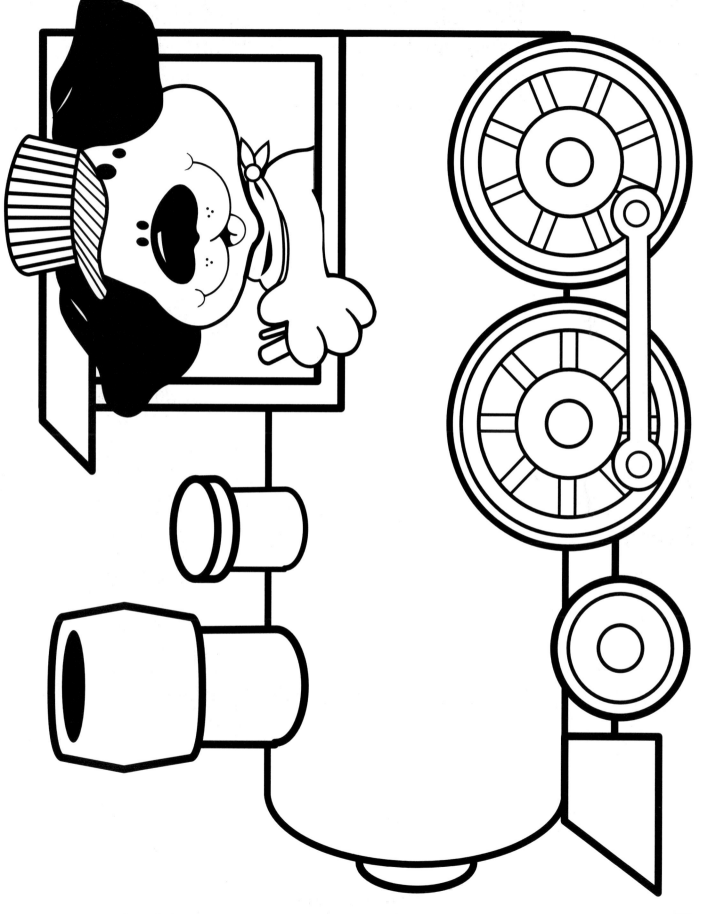

Pattern

Use with "Handwriting Across The USA" on page 18.

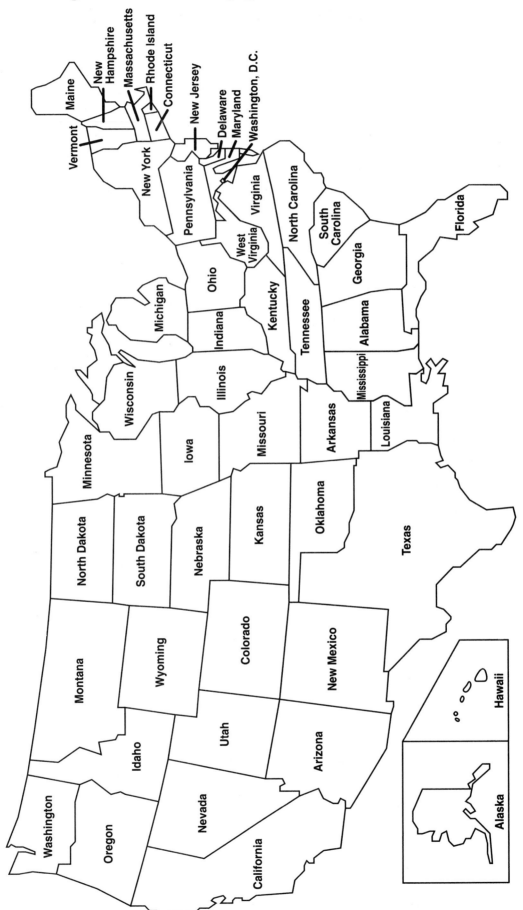

Abbreviations For The States

1. AL _____
2. AK _____
3. AZ _____
4. AR _____
5. CA _____
6. CO _____
7. CT _____
8. DE _____
9. FL _____
10. GA _____
11. HI _____
12. ID _____
13. IL _____
14. IN _____
15. IA _____
16. KS _____
17. KY _____
18. LA _____
19. ME _____
20. MD _____
21. MA _____
22. MI _____
23. MN _____
24. MS _____
25. MO _____

26. MT _____
27. NE _____
28. NV _____
29. NH _____
30. NJ _____
31. NM _____
32. NY _____
33. NC _____
34. ND _____
35. OH _____
36. OK _____
37. OR _____
38. PA _____
39. RI _____
40. SC _____
41. SD _____
42. TN _____
43. TX _____
44. UT _____
45. VT _____
46. VA _____
47. WA _____
48. DC _____
49. WV _____
50. WI _____
51. WY _____

Note To The Teacher: Use with "Handwriting Across The USA" on page 18.

Pattern
Use with " 'Hare-raising' Homophones" on page 19.

Pattern
Use with "Prefix Practice" on page 23.

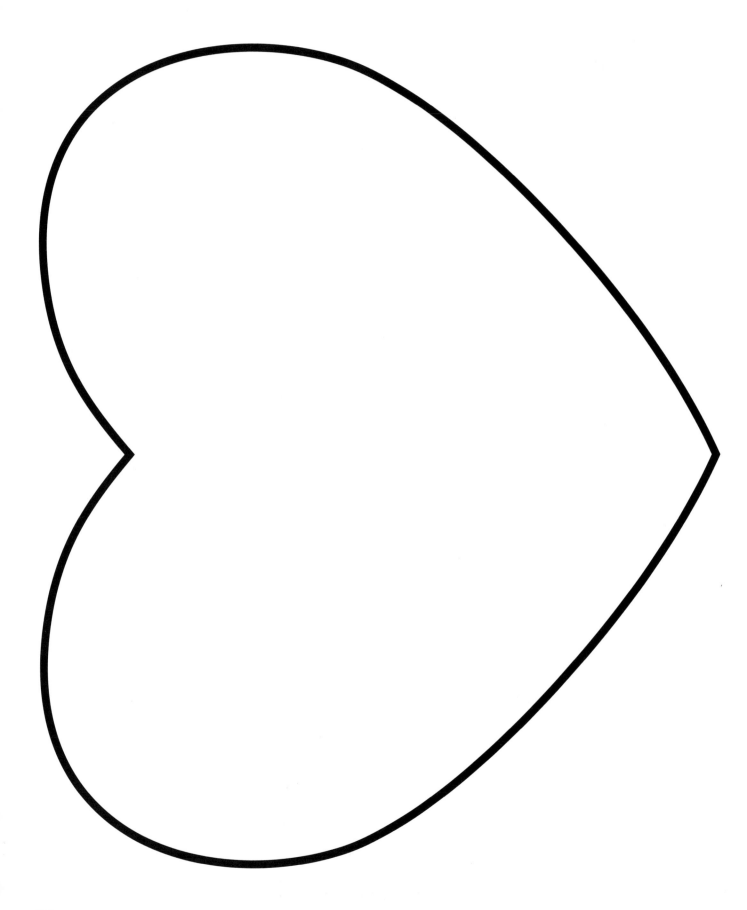

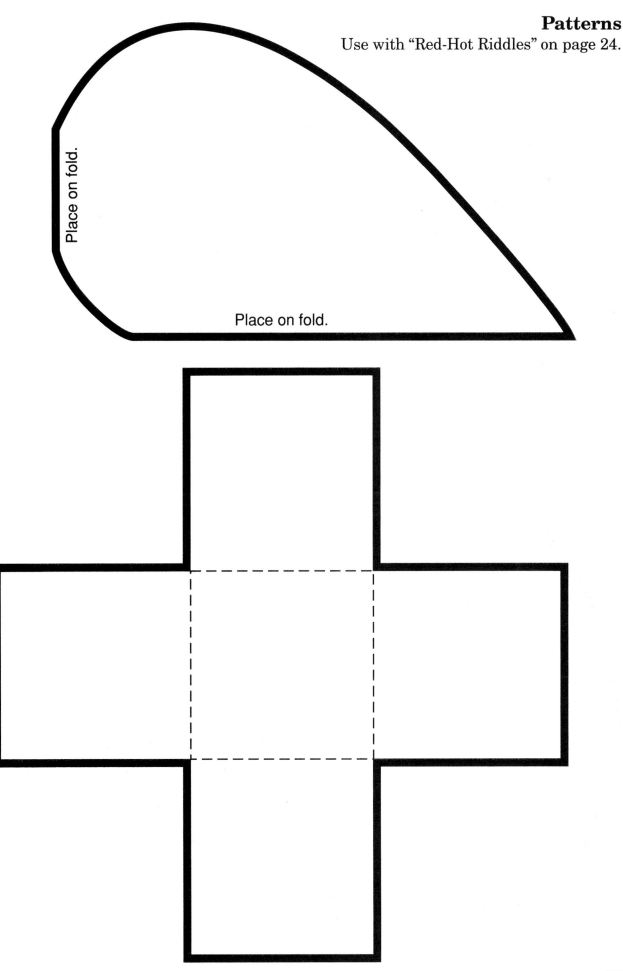

Place on fold.

Place on fold.

Pattern
Use with "Shamrock Synonyms" on page 28.

Pattern
Use with "Words-Go-Round" on page 29.

Pattern
Use with "Picture This!" on page 36.

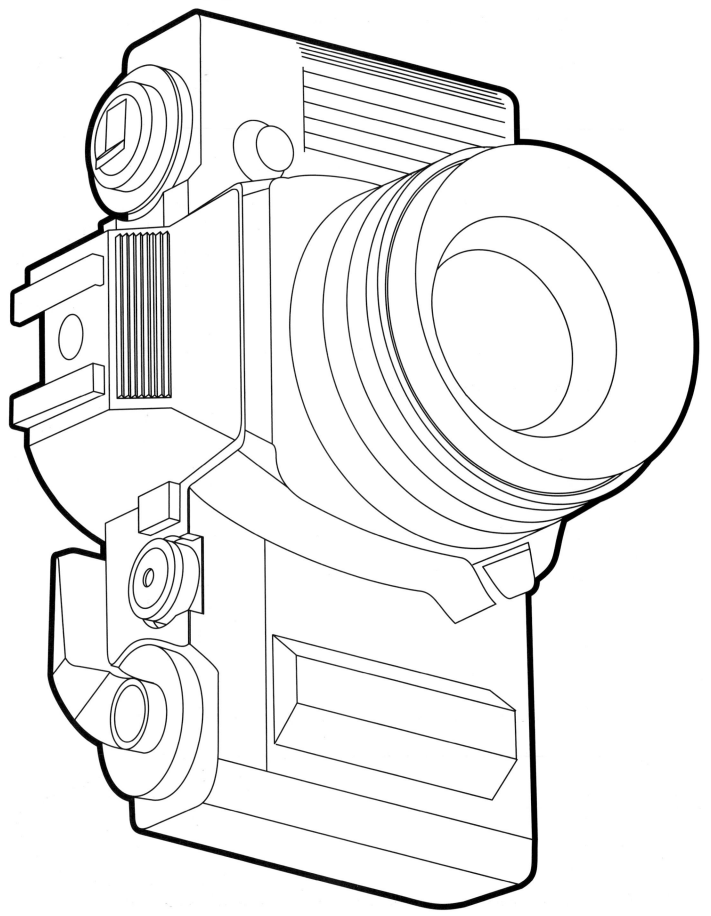

Use with "Colorful Creations" on page 36 and "Crayon Corner" on page 62.

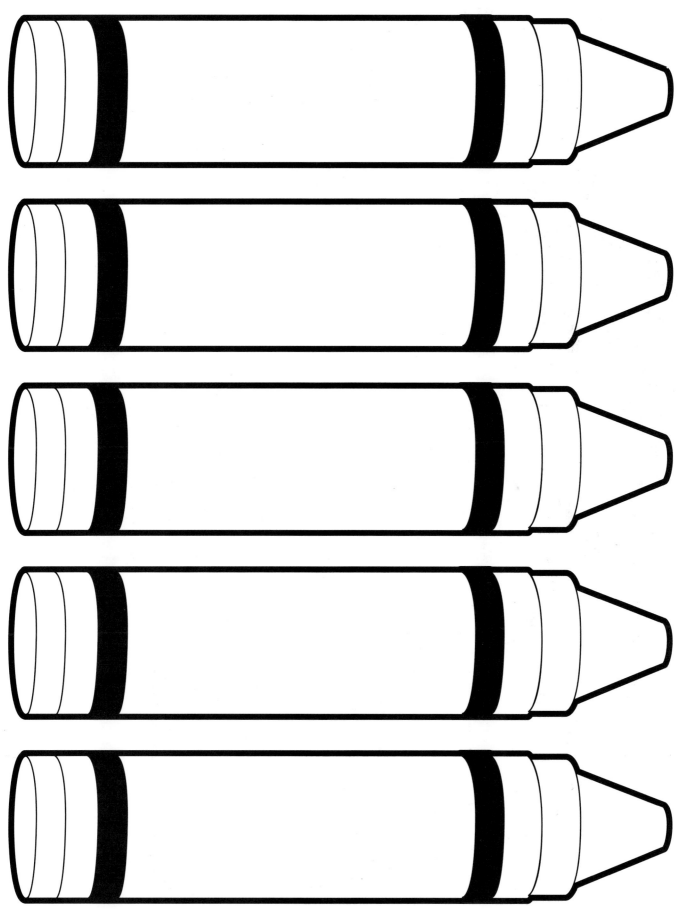

Patterns
Use with "Trimming The Tree" on page 38.

Correct

Incorrect

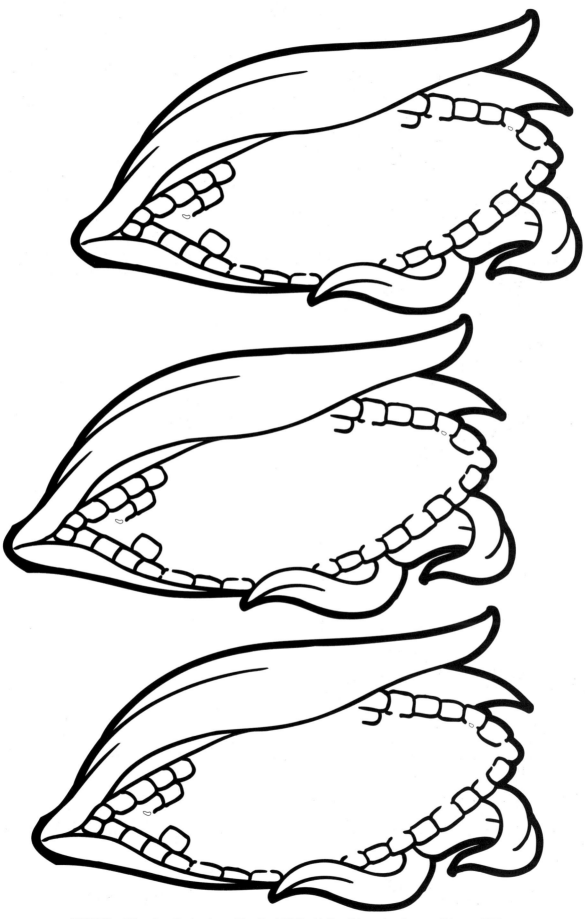

Patterns
Use with "Spider Math" on page 41.

Pattern
Use with "Getting To The Core!" on page 41.

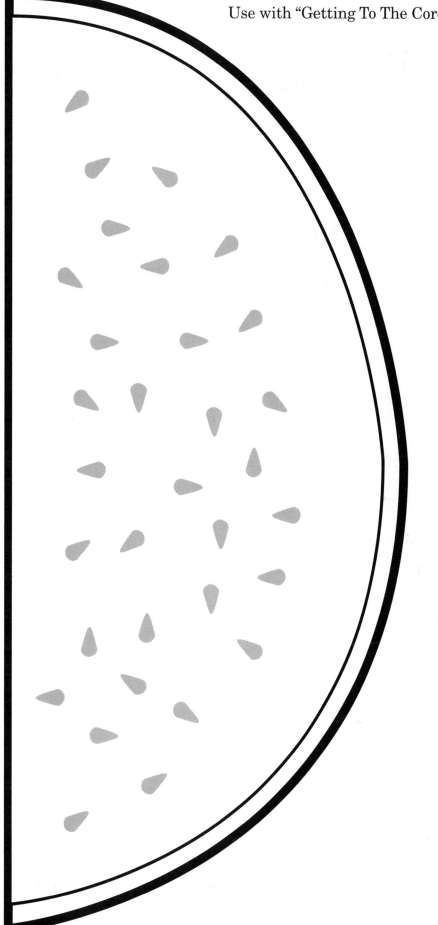

Patterns
Use with "Fill 'er Up!" on page 42.

1	2	3	4	5	6	7	8	9	10
11	12	13	14	15	16	17	18	19	20
21	22	23	24	25	26	27	28	29	30
31	32	33	34	35	36	37	38	39	40
41	42	43	44	45	46	47	48	49	50
51	52	53	54	55	56	57	58	59	60
61	62	63	64	65	66	67	68	69	70
71	72	73	74	75	76	77	78	79	80
81	82	83	84	85	86	87	88	89	90
91	92	93	94	95	96	97	98	99	100

Pattern
Use with "Pigging Out On Numbers" on page 44.

Fall Leaves

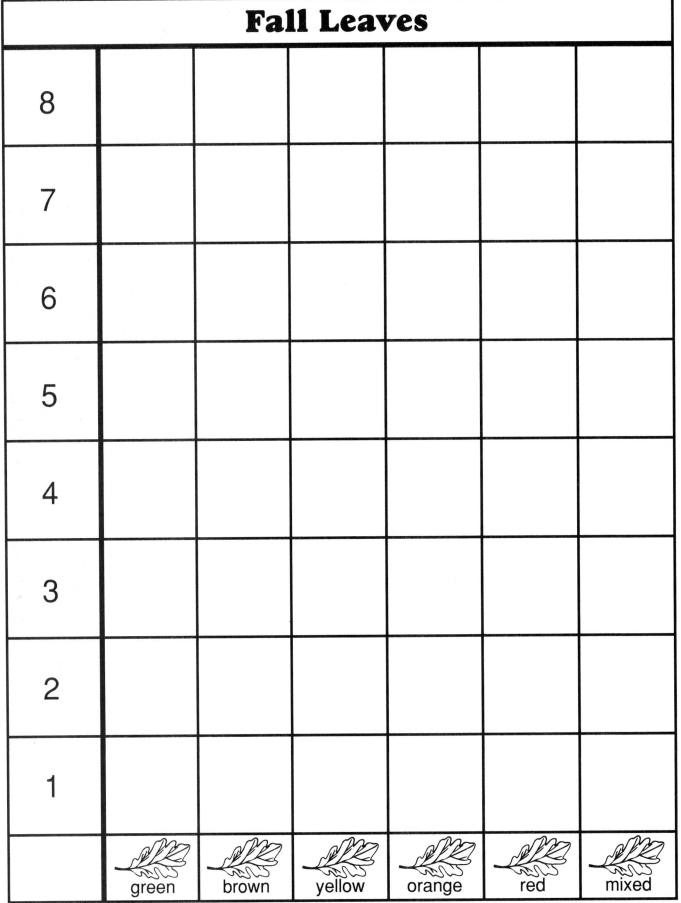

	green	brown	yellow	orange	red	mixed
8						
7						
6						
5						
4						
3						
2						
1						

Note To The Teacher: Use with "Falling For Leaves" on page 46.

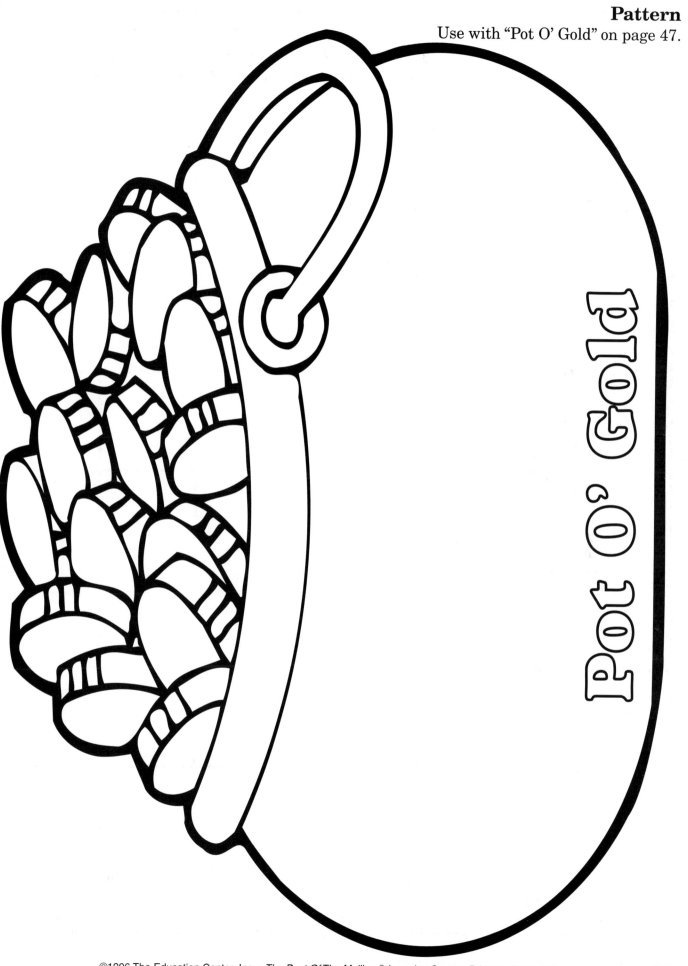

Pot O' Gold

Patterns
Use with Money Skills Activities on pages 49–51.

©1996 The Education Center, Inc. • *The Best Of* The Mailbox® *Learning Centers Primary* • TEC1455

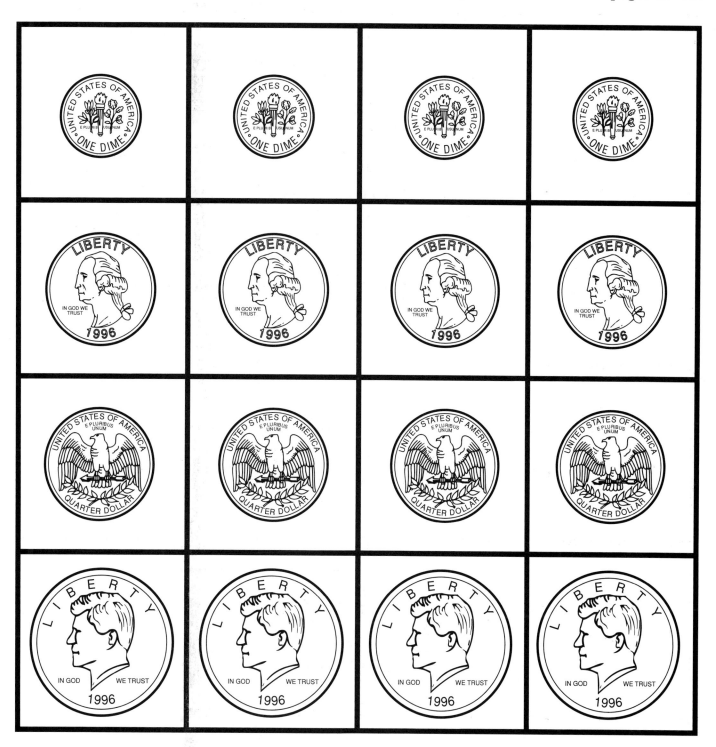

Patterns

Use with "Everything's A Dollar!" on page 51.

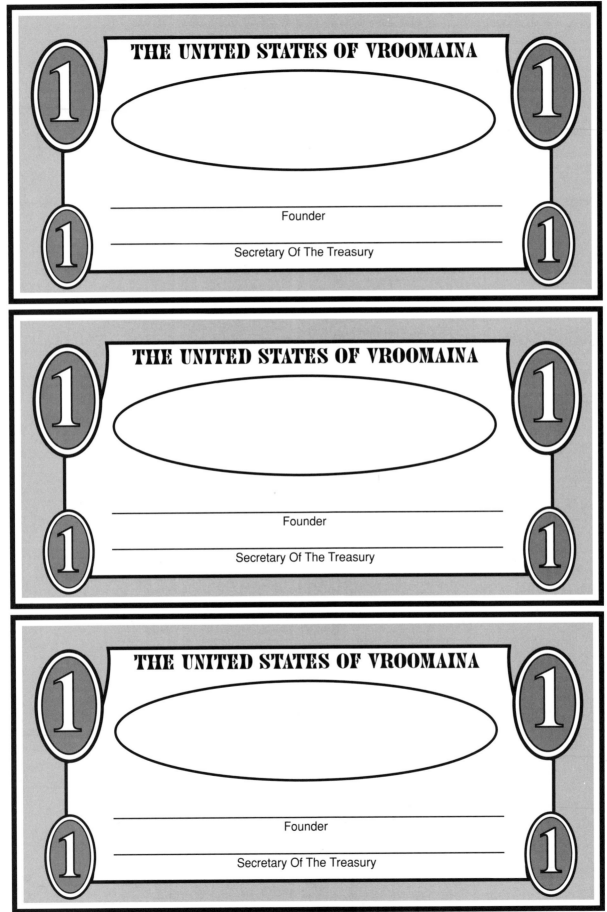

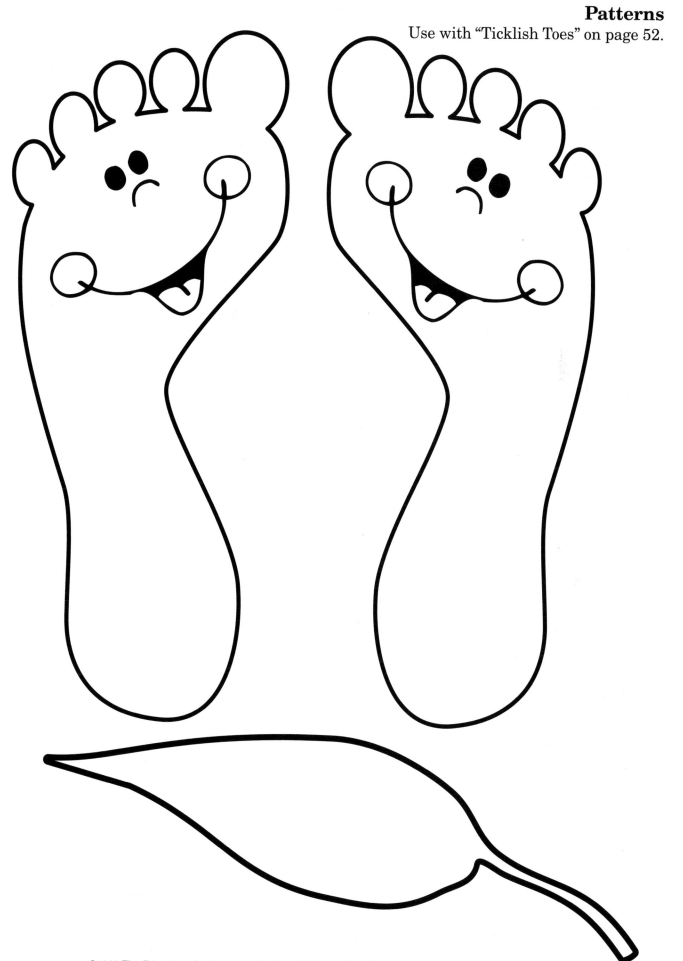

Pattern
Use with "Boo Juice" on page 52.

Cut on dotted line.

BOO JUICE

Pull the strip up.
Write the problem and answer.

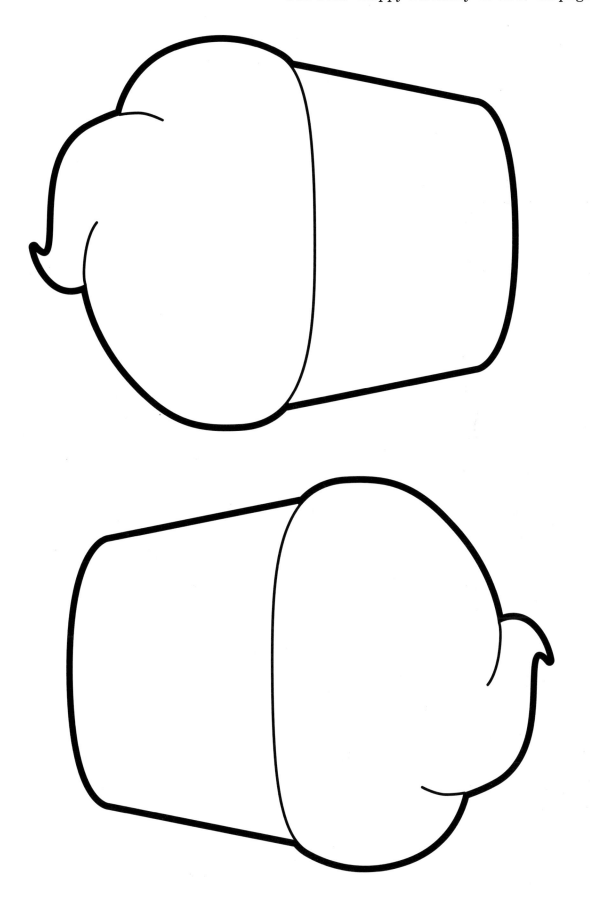

Patterns
Use with "Pocket Watch Practice" on page 56.

nose

ears

eyes

hat

eyes

Mr. Potato

bow tie

hat

ears

eyebrows

nose

bow tie

mouth

©1996 The Education Center, Inc. • *The Best Of The Mailbox® Learning Centers Primary* • TEC1455

Note To The Teacher: Use with " 'Tis Time To Draw" on page 60.

Pattern
Use with "Try Some Brew!" on page 63.

Name _____

Try Some Brew!

Color each picture when you have completed that folder's activity.

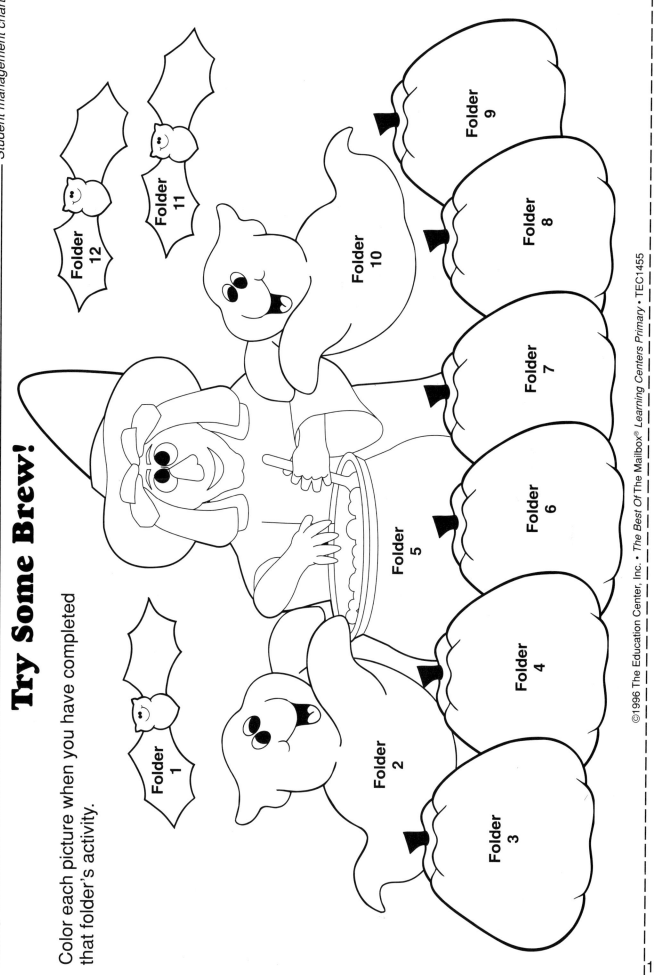

Note To The Teacher: Use with "Try Some Brew!" on page 63.

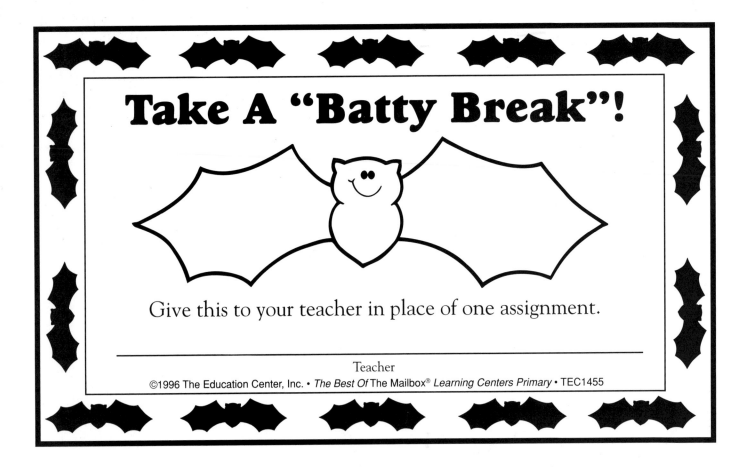

Take A "Batty Break"!

Give this to your teacher in place of one assignment.

_____
Teacher

©1996 The Education Center, Inc. • *The Best Of* The Mailbox® *Learning Centers Primary* • TEC1455

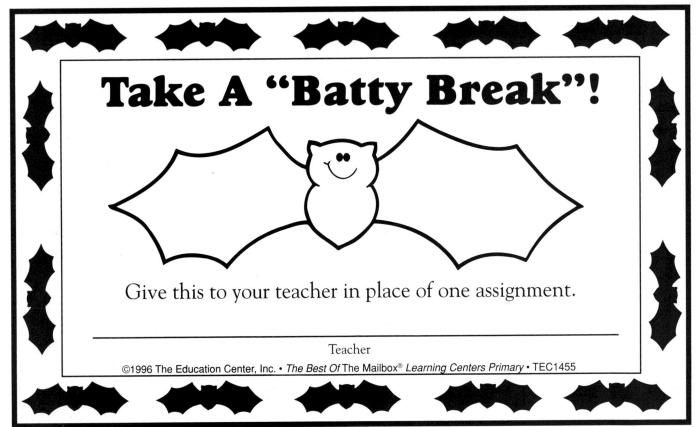

Take A "Batty Break"!

Give this to your teacher in place of one assignment.

_____
Teacher

©1996 The Education Center, Inc. • *The Best Of* The Mailbox® *Learning Centers Primary* • TEC1455

Patterns

Use with "Big Top Fun" on page 64.

Clip Art

שׁ ה נ נ

nun   gimel   hay   shin

Clip Art

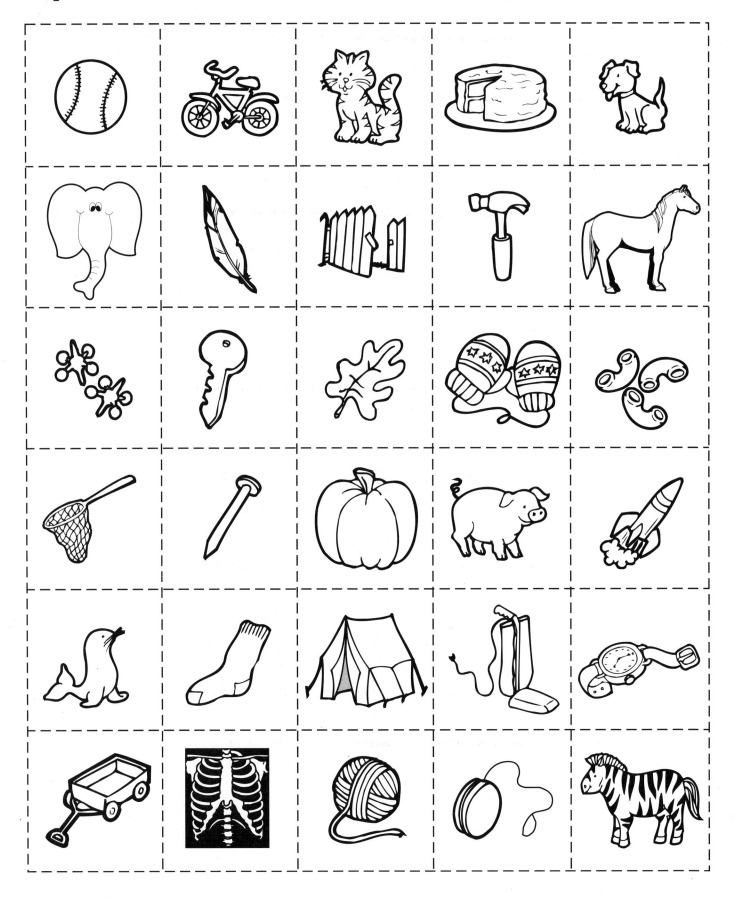